HOW TO MODIFY VOLKSWAGEN

BUS

SUSPENSION, BRAKES AND CHASSIS FOR HIGH PERFORMANCE

James Hale

VELOCE PUBLISHING
THE PUBLISHER OF FINE AUTOMOTIVE BOOKS

This book is dedicated to Francis and Christopher

SpeedPro Series
4-Cylinder Engine - How to Blueprint & Build a Short Block for High Performance by Des Hammill
Alfa Romeo Twin Cam Engines - How to Power Tune by Jim Kartalamakis
BMC 998cc A-Series Engine - How to Power Tune by Des Hammill
BMC/Rover 1275cc A-Series Engines - How to Power Tune by Des Hammill
Camshafts - How to Choose & Time them for Maximum Power by Des Hammill
Cylinder Heads - How to Build, Modify & Power Tune Updated & Revised Edition by Peter Burgess
Distributor-type Ignition Systems - How to Build & Power Tune by Des Hammill
Fast Road Car - How to Plan and Build New Edition by Daniel Stapleton
Ford SOHC 'Pinto' & Sierra Cosworth DOHC Engines - How to Power Tune Updated & Enlarged Edition by Des Hammill
Ford V8 - How to Power Tune Small Block Engines by Des Hammill
Harley-Davidson Evolution Engines - How to Build & Power Tune by Des Hammill
Holley Carburetors - How to Build & Power Tune New Edition by Des Hammill
Jaguar XK Engines - How to Power Tune New Edition by Des Hammill
MG Midget & Austin-Healey Sprite - How to Power Tune Updated Edition by Daniel Stapleton
MGB 4-Cylinder Engine - How to Power Tune by Peter Burgess
MGB - How to Give your MGB V8 Power Updated & Revised Edition by Roger Williams
MGB, MGC & MGB V8 - How to Improve by Roger Williams
Mini Engines - How to Power Tune on a Small Budget 2nd Edition by Des Hammill
Motorsport - Getting Started in by SS Collins
Nitrous Oxide Systems - How to Build & Power Tune by Trevor Langfield
Rover V8 Engines - How to Power Tune by Des Hammill
Sportscar/Kitcar Suspension & Brakes - How to Build & Modify Enlarged & Updated 2nd Edition by Des Hammill
SU Carburettors - How to Build & Modify for High Performance by Des Hammill
Suzuki 4WD for Serious Offroad Action - Modifying by John Richardson
Tiger Avon Sportscar - How to Build Your Own Updated & Revised 2nd Edition by Jim Dudley
TR2, 3 & TR4 - How to Improve by Roger Williams
TR5, 250 & TR6 - How to Improve by Roger Williams
V8 Engine - How to Build a Short Block for High Performance by Des Hammill
Volkswagen Beetle Suspension, Brakes & Chassis - How to Modify for High Performance by James Hale
Volkswagen Bus Suspension, Brakes & Chassis - How to Modify for High Performance by James Hale
Weber DCOE, & Dellorto DHLA Carburetors - How to Build & Power Tune 3rd Edition by Des Hammill

Those were the days ... Series
Alpine Trials & Rallies 1910-1973 by Martin Pfundner
Austerity Motoring by Malcolm Bobbitt
Brighton National Speed Trials by Tony Gardiner
British Police Cars by Nick Walker
Crystal Palace by Sam Collins
Dune Buggy Phenomenon by James Hale
More Dune Buggies by James Hale
Motor Racing at Brands Hatch in the Seventies by Chas Parker
Motor Racing at Goodwood in the Sixties by Tony Gardiner
Three Wheelers by Malcolm Bobbitt

Enthusiast's Restoration Manual Series
Citroen 2CV - How to Restore by Lindsay Porter
Classic Car Body Work - How to Restore by Martin Thaddeus
Classic Cars - How to Paint by Martin Thaddeus
Reliant Regal - How to Restore by Elvis Payne
Triumph TR2/3/3A - How to Restore by Roger Williams
Triumph TR4/4A - How to Restore by Roger Williams
Triumph TR5/250 & 6 - How to Restore by Roger Williams
Triumph TR7/8 - How to Restore by Roger Williams
Volkswagen Beetle - How to Restore by Jim Tyler

Essential Buyer's Guide Series
Alfa GT Buyer's Guide by Keith Booker
Alfa Romeo Giulia Spider Buyer's Guide by Keith Booker
Jaguar E-Type Buyer's Guide
Porsche 928 Buyer's Guide by David Hemmings
VW Beetle Buyer's Guide by Ken Cservenka & Richard Copping

Auto Graphics Series
Fiat & Abarth by Andrea & David Sparrow
Jaguar MkII by Andrea & David Sparrow
Lambretta LI by Andrea & David Sparrow

General
AC Two-litre Saloons & Buckland Sportscars by Leo Archibald
Alfa Romeo Berlinas (Saloons/Sedans) by John Tipler
Alfa Romeo Giulia Coupé GT & GTA by John Tipler
Alfa Tipo 33 Development, Racing & Chassis History by Ed McDonough
Anatomy of the Works Minis by Brian Moylan
Armstrong-Siddeley by Bill Smith
Autodrome by Sam Collins & Gavin Ireland
Automotive A-Z, Lane's Dictionary of Automotive Terms by Keith Lane
Automotive Mascots by David Kay & Lynda Springate
Bentley Continental, Corniche and Azure by Martin Bennett
BMCs Competition Department Secrets by Stuart Turner, Peter Browning & Marcus Chambers
BMW 5-Series by Marc Cranswick
BMW Z-Cars by James Taylor
British 250cc Racing Motorcycles by Chris Pereira
British Cars, The Complete Catalogue of, 1895-1975 by Culshaw & Horrobin

Bugatti Type 40 by Barrie Price
Bugatti 46/50 Updated Edition by Barrie Price
Bugatti 57 2nd Edition by Barrie Price
Caravans, The Illustrated History 1919-1959 by Andrew Jenkinson
Caravans, The Illustrated History from 1960 by Andrew Jenkinson
Chrysler 300 - America's Most Powerful Car 2nd Edition by Robert Ackerson
Citroën DS by Malcolm Bobbitt
Cobra - The Real Thing! by Trevor Legate
Cortina - Ford's Bestseller by Graham Robson
Coventry Climax Racing Engines by Des Hammill
Daimler SP250 'Dart' by Brian Long
Datsun 240, 260 & 280Z by Brian Long
Dune Buggy Files by James Hale
Dune Buggy Handbook by James Hale
Fiat & Abarth 124 Spider & Coupé by John Tipler
Fiat & Abarth 500 & 600 2nd Edition by Malcolm Bobbitt
Ford F100/F150 Pick-up 1948-1996 by Robert Ackerson
Ford F150 1997-2005 by Robert Ackerson
Ford GT40 by Trevor Legate
Ford Model Y by Sam Roberts
Funky Mopeds by Richard Skelton
Honda NSX Supercar by Brian Long
Jaguar, the Rise of by Barrie Price
Jaguar XJ-S by Brian Long
Jeep CJ by Robert Ackerson
Jeep Wrangler by Robert Ackerson
Karmann-Ghia Coupé & Convertible by Malcolm Bobbitt
Land Rover, The Half-Ton Military by Mark Cook
Lea-Francis Story, The by Barrie Price
Lexus Story, The by Brian Long
Lola - The Illustrated History (1957-1977) by John Starkey
Lola - All The Sports Racing & Single-Seater Racing Cars 1978-1997 by John Starkey
Lola T70 - The Racing History & Individual Chassis Record 3rd Edition by John Starkey
Lotus 49 by Michael Oliver
Marketingmobiles, The Wonderful Wacky World of, James Hale
Mazda MX-5/Miata 1.6 Enthusiast's Workshop Manual by Rod Grainger & Pete Shoemark
Mazda MX-5/Miata 1.8 Enthusiast's Workshop Manual by Rod Grainger & Pete Shoemark
Mazda MX-5 (& Eunos Roadster) - The World's Favourite Sportscar by Brian Long
Mazda MX-5 Miata Roadster by Brian Long
MGA by John Price Williams
MGB & MGB GT - Expert Guide (Auto-Doc Series) by Roger Williams
Micro Caravans by Andrew Jenkinson
Mini Cooper - The Real Thing! by John Tipler
Mitsubishi Lancer Evo by Brian Long
Motor Racing Reflections by Anthony Carter
Motorhomes, The Illustrated History by Andrew Jenkinson
Motorsport in colour, 1950s by Martyn Wainwright
MR2 - Toyota's Mid-engined Sports Car by Brian Long
Nissan 300ZX & 350Z - The Z-Car Story by Brian Long
Pass Your Theory & Practical Driving Tests by Clive Gibson & Gavin Hoole
Pontiac Firebird by Marc Cranswick
Porsche Boxster by Brian Long
Porsche 356 by Brian Long
Porsche 911 Carrera by Tony Corlett
Porsche 911R, RS & RSR, 4th Edition by John Starkey
Porsche 911 - The Definitive History 1963-1971 by Brian Long
Porsche 911 - The Definitive History 1971-1977 by Brian Long
Porsche 911 - The Definitive History 1977-1987 by Brian Long
Porsche 911 - The Definitive History 1987-1997 by Brian Long
Porsche 911 - The Definitive History 1997-2004 by Brian Long
Porsche 911SC 'Super Carrera' by Adrian Streather
Porsche 914 & 914-6 by Brian Long
Porsche 924 by Brian Long
Porsche 933 'King of Porsche' by Adrian Streather
Porsche 944 by Brian Long
RAC Rally Action! by Tony Gardiner
Rolls-Royce Silver Shadow/Bentley T Series Corniche & Camargue Revised & Enlarged Edition by Malcolm Bobbitt
Rolls-Royce Silver Spirit, Silver Spur & Bentley Mulsanne 2nd Edition by Malcolm Bobbitt
Rolls-Royce Silver Wraith, Dawn & Cloud/Bentley MkVI, R & S Series by Martyn Nutland
RX-7 - Mazda's Rotary Engine Sportscar (updated & revised new Edition) by Brian Long
Singer Story: Cars, Commercial Vehicles, Bicycles & Motorcycles by Kevin Atkinson
Subaru Impreza by Brian Long
Taxi! The Story of the 'London' Taxicab by Malcolm Bobbitt
Triumph Motorcycles & the Meriden Factory by Hughie Hancox
Triumph Speed Twin & Thunderbird Bible by Harry Woolridge
Triumph Tiger Cub Bible by Mike Estall
Triumph Trophy Bible by Harry Woolridge
Triumph TR6 by William Kimberley
Turner's Triumphs, Edward Turner & his Triumph Motorcycles by Jeff Clew
Velocette Motorcycles - MSS to Thruxton Updated & Revised Edition by Rod Burris
Volkswagen Bus or Van to Camper, How to Convert by Lindsay Porter
Volkswagens of the World by Simon Glen
VW Beetle Cabriolet by Malcolm Bobbitt
VW Beetle - The Car of the 20th Century by Richard Copping
VW Bus, Camper, Van, Pickup by Malcolm Bobbitt
VW - The air-cooled era by Richard Copping
Works Rally Mechanic by Brian Moylan

First published in 2003. Reprinted 2005 by Veloce Publishing Ltd., 33 Trinity Street, Dorchester DT1 1TT, England.
Fax 01305 268864/e-mail info@veloce.co.uk/web www.veloce.co.uk or www.velocebooks.com
ISBN 1-903706-14-9/UPC 36847-00214-5

Readers with ideas for automotive books, or books on other transport or related hobby subjects, are invited to write to the editorial director of Veloce Publishing Ltd. at the above address.

British Library Cataloguing in Publication Data -
A catalogue record for this book is available from the British Library.
Typesetting, design and page make-up all by Veloce Publishing Ltd. on Apple Mac.
Printed in India

Contents

Veloce SpeedPro books -

ISBN 1 903706 76 9

ISBN 1 903706 91 2

ISBN 1 903706 77 7

ISBN 1 903706 78 5

ISBN 1 901295 73 7

ISBN 1 903706 75 0

ISBN 1 901295 62 1

ISBN 1 874105 70 7

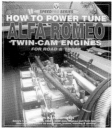
ISBN 1 903706 60 2

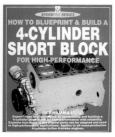
ISBN 1 903706 92 0

ISBN 1 903706 94 7

ISBN 1 901295 26 5

ISBN 1 901295 07 9

ISBN 1 903706 59 9

ISBN 1 903706 73 4

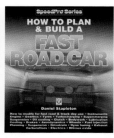
ISBN 1 904788 78-5

ISBN 1 901295 76 1

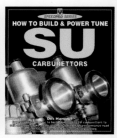
ISBN 1 903706 98 X

ISBN 1 903706 99 8

ISBN 1 84584 005 4

ISBN 1-904788-84-X

ISBN 1-904788-22-X

ISBN 1 903706 17 3

ISBN 1 84584 006 2

ISBN 1 903706 80 7

ISBN 1 903706 68 8

ISBN 1 903706 14 9

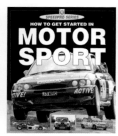
ISBN 1 903706 70 X

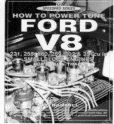
ISBN 1 903706 72 6

- more on the way!

Introduction & Acknowledgements

INTRODUCTION

The VW Transporter has become a motoring icon across the world during the long time it has been in production. Introduced at the end of the 1940s as a workhorse to transport materials around the VW factory, the design was soon developed into a much needed commercial vehicle. The Transporter, like the Beetle before it, was to help rebuild commerce and industry in Germany's war-torn aftermath and then go on to become an international best-seller.

To many the Transporter has become not just a means of transport, but a way of life. Introduced at a time when there were few other commercial vehicles available, its strength, dependability, and sheer go anywhere characteristics have all been fundamental to its universal success. Since those early days, the design has been progressively updated to meet

Three generations of air-cooled VW Transporter. (Courtesy Walter Bach)

the demands and expectations of the buying public, and four generations of Transporters have now been

1954 Micro-Bus Deluxe showed the style of VW's Transporter to perfection.

**Commercially successful, the Transporter travelled the world in both van and camper-van designs.
(Courtesy John Jackson)**

Since the vehicle was designed to fulfil a utilitarian role, it might come as a surprise that the earlier Split-screen and Bay-window design Transporters (or Buses, as they have also become widely known), have gained such a cult status throughout the world. Besides being the ultimate 'box on wheels' for small businesses (as VW itself promoted it), it provided a superb way to advertise a business on the flat side panels. However, it was as a camper-van that the Transporter was to gain its legendary status. Here was a low-cost vehicle that was as comfortable to drive as a saloon car and had the same wheelbase as a Beetle (which could be driven by anyone). You could take the whole family away for holiday breaks

tune the vehicle. The Transporter was never conceived as a 'performance' vehicle, so it might seem somewhat contradictory to write a book about how to modify the design for 'high performance'. Nevertheless, the performance parts' market for the Transporter - so often overshadowed by that for the Beetle - has positively flourished in the last few years. This can be attributed, in part, to the general interest in the earlier VW designs, and also to the improved quality of manufacture and availability of aftermarket parts. Because of this growth in global marketing I have tried to include suppliers from many countries including the USA, the UK, Germany and Australia.

produced. The more angular panels of the modern 'T4', with its front-mounted, water-cooled engine, may have replaced the 'friendly' face and rear-mounted, air-cooled engine of the

**Cutaway, showing the Transporter's interior, and engineering vitals.
(Courtesy Malcolm Bobbitt)**

**Like the Beetle, the Transporter's basic swing axle suspension could cause problems for the unwary!
(Courtesy Gemeente-archief Rotterdam)**

early Split-screen design. However, the concept of providing economical transport and VW quality is still the same.

in it without the inconveniences of hitching up a separate caravan. It really was a home-from-home that could be driven anywhere! Generations of families, and those travelling the globe, have all come to love the VW Transporter. Indeed it can be seen as the forerunner of today's MPVs (Multi-Purpose Vehicles).

Unlike the Beetle, the Transporter is a much less obvious choice for those wishing to modify, customise or

This book is substantially different to other VW Bus/Transporter books. I have not focused on the history of the marque, except to describe design changes and developments. Neither have I provided information on buying a Transporter, restoring it to its original specification, or converting it into a camper-van. Those areas are already well catered for, and there's little point duplicating what already exists. Instead, the areas this book covers are purely concerned with the brake and suspension systems components and the design of the 'chassis' and underpinnings of the vehicles. Here's a guide to those owners who are hoping to get the best from their Transporter's suspension and brakes, and are confident enough to tackle modification or maintenance jobs. The book doesn't replace a good workshop manual (you should still have one of those available), but it is complementary in its detail.

With the Transporter things are more complicated than with the Beetle. The most obvious consideration is its sheer size and weight. Being a commercial vehicle, the components that make up items like the front suspension are physically bigger, and consequently heavier, than on a normal car. On some occasions this will mean having someone to help you when removing or refitting components, and having the right equipment to lift the vehicle, and work under it safely. I'll provide more advice in the section on tools and safety. There are also times when welding will be required, and specialist help may need to be sought.

Overall, though, the design isn't entirely dissimilar to that of a Beetle. I've always found that the best way to understand vehicle mechanics is to consider individual systems on the vehicle, rather than trying to understand at once the way everything works. For instance, you can divide the Transporter into areas such as the braking system, steering system, fuel system, ignition system, suspension system and so on. Looking at them separately greatly helps anyone, with a basic knowledge of mechanics, to understand how they work. From there it's only a short step to understanding how they can be improved to enhance performance.

Current interest in the VW Bus has spawned a whole performance aftermarket for enthusiasts.
(Courtesy Alex Leighton)

The choice of components doesn't have to be limited to the VW factory to achieve performance. Aftermarket suppliers have paved the way for many of the modifications that you'll see in this book. You need to move away from the confines of thinking 'purely VW parts' to get the best for

Shortened Split-screen Bus proves there's no limit to an owner's imagination.
(Courtesy Alex Leighton)

your bus. Be broad-minded, and think laterally. For instance, if you wish to fit alloy wheels to your newly installed brake drums, or discs, you don't necessarily have to follow what's gone before. Providing you can find alloys with a suitable bolt pattern, hubs can be re-drilled. There's also a flourishing market in wheel adaptors that will allow a huge range of different wheels to be fitted to your Bus. Such opportunities enable you to get the best performance and looks from your vehicle, at a realistic cost, and make your Bus stand out in a crowd.

Limo Bus concept stretches the original Transporter design to an extreme.

French look custom crew cab with wild graphics and alloy wheels. (Courtesy Mike Key)

Even as a VW driver, mechanic and devotee of many years' standing one of the hardest things to understand, at first, was the 'coded' language that other enthusiasts use when talking about their vehicles. There are many different 'Types' of design, and different models within those ranges, so I feel it's worth detailing the references that will be made within this book. I've used the term 'Bus' on the front cover, and I've used it in the text to avoid repeating the word Transporter, but I've often debated exactly what the correct name should be for these vehicles. The term 'Bus' is well known in the USA, Germany and France, but in other parts of the world they are more commonly known as 'Kombi' or 'Kombi-van' (South Africa and Australia), or 'Combi' (Brazil and Mexico). In Germany, the term Kombi refers to an empty panel van. In Mexico a 'Caravelle' is a Bay-window Bus, and not (as you might expect) a 'Third generation' or 'Wedge' Bus. Even this latter term is confusing, as the shape is more brick-like than a wedge.

In the UK, 'Bus' is well known, although they are often referred to as Type 2s. Then again, camper-van manufacturers' names such as 'Dormobile' or 'Devon' are sometimes used regardless of whether they have camping interiors or are merely empty panel vans. In the USA, the

terms 'Microbus', 'Station Wagon', 'Vanagon' and 'Eurovan' are common. Even using the generic term 'Type 2' can be problematic, because the fourth generation vehicle (T4), with front-wheel drive, should correctly be referred to as a 'Type 70'. Also, use of the term 'Type 25' for the third generation vehicles (T3) is well known, but it can also cause confusion since a 'Type 25' is also a version of the (T1) Split-screen Microbus or Samba (with additional windows mounted at roof level). The pick-up version of the third generation vehicles is also officially a 'Type 24'.

So you can see the problem. I've drawn the conclusion that the word 'Bus' covers most eventualities, but also that 'Transporter' solves a myriad of identity and name problems. Volkswagen intended the term 'Transporter' to apply to all, and it ultimately helps distinguish between the four Transporter generations. T1, T2, T3 and T4 refer to Transporter 1, Transporter 2, Transporter 3,

Suspension lowering, bright paintwork and alloy wheels keeps the Transporter looking modern. (Courtesy Tobias Lindback)

and Transporter 4, and not merely 'Type', as is so often used. As 'Type' is often abbreviated to 'T', this also adds confusion with other VW models such as the Type 3 range (Variant/Squareback, Fastback and Notchback), and the Type 4 range (VW 411 and 412).

So, having concluded that Bus/Transporter are the best words to refer to such VWs as a range of vehicles, I will also use the most common names in VW parlance to describe the models. A first generation Bus (T1) is best known as a Split-screen Bus, regardless of what model it actually is. A second generation Bus (T2) is usually referred to as a Bay-window Bus, with the same proviso. A third generation Bus (T3) de facto is most often called a Type 25 or, in the UK, a Wedge Bus. A fourth generation Bus (T4) is called (thankfully) a T4.

Split-screen Bus becomes a drag-racer with a hot motor, and 'wheelie' bars. (Courtesy Rob Hallstrom)

Bay-window Bus smokes the rear tyres during a burn-out on the drag strip. (Courtesy Paul Knight).

Whatever type of VW Bus you own, I'm sure you will find something within these pages to inspire you to improve its braking or suspension performance. You may want to just keep it stock, but renew worn parts, so that your Bus will be safer and more enjoyable to drive. Or, you may want to lower or raise the suspension and up-rate its braking performance to create a truly unique vehicle. There are plenty of possibilities.

Read on. Your Bus will love you for it!

James Hale
Brighton, England.

Early T1 Split-screen Transporter can be transformed into a Baja Bus for serious off-road use. (Courtesy Simon Glen)

Having got the different generations of VW Bus finally worked out, I should point out that it's specifically the T1 and T2 that I'll be looking at in depth. The T3 (Type 25) rear suspension will also be mentioned as it uses a similar constant velocity joint (CV) and driveshaft arrangement at the rear to the later T2 design. The T4 is a radical departure from the previous rear-engine designs and will not be covered.

T2 Bay-window transporter is ready for pavement cruising with 2-litre air-cooled engine, lowered suspension, and alloy wheels. (Courtesy Simon Glen)

ACKNOWLEDGEMENTS

To produce a book that attempts a new 'slant' on a marque that's so well known, and which has endeared itself to generations of enthusiasts, is a challenge beyond belief. I am deeply indebted to the many VW Bus enthusiasts, around the world, who provided me with so much information and photography. The complete enthusiasm and love of their vehicles shone through at every opportunity. Their knowledge, skill and sheer friendliness knew no bounds, and I enjoyed every moment with them both as an observer and learner during the project, and as a friend long after the book was completed. Thank you all for your help in so many ways.

To: Walter Bach, Malcolm Bobbitt, John Jackson, Tobias Lindback, Jon Betts, Rob Hallstrom, John Clewer, Mike Key, Paul Utting, Richard Parsons, Jon Smith, Alex Leighton, Ivan McCutcheon and Paul Knight at Volksworld magazine, Simon Pollock at Nefarious Design, Wayne Tyas and Ian at Volksheaven, Mark Cornwall at Car Parts Direct, Mark Reynolds at Just Kampers, Simon Skelding at Red 9 Design and Mark Richards for providing photography.

To: Richard Foks at Bluebird Customs, and Big Boys Toys for providing parts for photography.

To: Rod Sleigh at VW Books; Bob at BBT in Belgium, Robert Meekings and Chris Tasker at the Split-screen Van Club, for help and advice and generally pointing me in the right direction.

To: Dave & Mandy Palmer at Creative Engineering, Thomas Kelm at Custom & Speed Parts, Kimm Garland at Indian Automotive, and Mike Kristen at Custom Bugs & Buses for their time, help, and specialist advice on all Bus-related matters, and for arranging photography without which this book would never have happened.

I am indebted to Simon Glen for once again helping me out with his unique knowledge of the complexities of the VW chassis and gearbox numbering systems and model designations; for providing photography from his extensive collection and for arranging to photograph Buses and parts 'down under'. Thanks Simon.

What is it?

Glad you asked.
It's a Volkswagen Station Wagon
Don't pity the poor thing; it can take it.
It can carry nearly a ton of anything you can afford to buy.
Or 8 people (plus luggage) if you want to get practical about it.
And there's more than one practical consideration.
It will take you about 24 miles on a gallon of regular gas.
It won't take any water or anti-freeze at all; the engine is air-cooled.
And even though it carries almost twice as much as regular wagons, it takes 4 feet less to park.
What's in the package?
8 pairs of skis, the complete works of Dickens, 98 lbs. of frozen spinach, a hutch used by Grover Cleveland, 80 Hollywood High gym sweaters, a suit of armor, and a full sized reproduction of the Winged Victory of Samothrace.

10

Workshop procedures, safety & tools

WORKSHOP PROCEDURES & SAFETY

There's always a temptation to rush into working on something without firstly reading the instructions - especially where vehicles are concerned. If you read no instructions or heed no other advice before working on your VW Bus, read and remember this one thing: you are working on a big and heavy vehicle.

It's stating the obvious, I know, but it is amazing just how many enthusiasts will rush headlong into the mechanical work on their Bus without really taking this fundamental point into consideration. From a practical point of view this means two things. Firstly, to work on it indoors in the comfort of a clean and dry area means that you'll need a big (and tall) garage, outhouse, industrial unit, or something similar. Secondly, you'll need assistance when it comes to moving the larger items, such as the front suspension or transaxle, due to

their sheer weight, and you'll need equipment like a trolley jack and axle stands that are strong enough to respectively lift and support the weight of such items. The VW Bus weighs over one ton (975kg) in total (unladen), and that's pretty evenly spread between the engine, transaxle and fuel tank weight at the rear, and the suspension components up front. In use, with a driver and front seat passenger in situ, the weight is perfectly balanced front to rear. However, whilst there will probably be no occupants in the Bus when you're working on it, this is something to bear in mind!

If you've access to a garage, or at least a dry and clean storage area, this will not only make working on the Bus more pleasant, but will also help prevent rust forming on mechanical components or repair panels. If you're planning a long-term restoration project, or the major rebuild of certain areas of the Bus, this is something to consider.

Make sure that whatever space you have available allows you to work around the Bus, with enough space above so it can be jacked up. If you've a pit to work in and get underneath the vehicle, so much the better. To allow a safe and clean area, on which to dismantle components, a strong workbench is a must, whilst a separate storage area for tools and parts is a good idea. Dry storage of tools - especially power tools - is simply common sense, and all tools should be stored away after use for their longevity and your safety.

There are other obvious safety issues. Firstly, don't smoke anywhere near a flammable liquid, such as petrol or brake fluid. Brake fluid is often overlooked, but it is highly flammable, as well as corrosive to paintwork, your eyes and skin. Petrol vapour can also be underestimated, as it is this - rather than just the liquid - that is combustible. Even when a fuel tank is drained, it is still dangerous if you have a heat source nearby (such as when welding), so be prepared to remove the tank from the working area.

Secondly, always wear safety clothing, including goggles, if you are cutting and grinding with power tools. Gloves will help prevent the inevitable cuts and grazes from sharp metal objects or edges. They also keep you clean when removing dirty and greasy components from the vehicle. A breathing mask prevents the inhalation of harmful brake dust that may collect in the drums. Although there is probably no asbestos particles from the friction material these days, any dust that comes out of the brake drums should be carefully disposed of. Avoid contacting the brake friction surfaces with grease or oil from your hands, as this will contaminate them, and reduce brake efficiency.

I've mentioned the importance of robust axle stands earlier, and these are essential if you're to observe the golden rule of mechanics - Never work under an unsupported car (or Bus). Bricks, wooden blocks or makeshift stands shouldn't even be considered for a VW Bus, let alone anything else. Beg, borrow or hire the proper stands for this job, and make sure they are positioned correctly under strength members of the Bus. Get it wrong and that one-ton weight could end up on top of you - you have been warned ...

That's enough horror stories about the weight; now let's think about the components you'll be rebuilding and replacing. As items are removed for inspection and modification, remember to thoroughly clean them in a proprietary cleaning agent. This not only makes them more pleasant to work on, but also prevents the ingress of dirt into precision surfaces as they are stripped down completely. Upon reassembly or refitting, use of a copper-based lubricant on items,

such as bolt threads or components that require adjustment, will also make future disassembly or movement easier. The exception to this is on components that are set to a specific torque, and where the friction of the fit between the components must not be reduced by the use of such lubricants. Torqued components could otherwise be over-stressed as they are fitted. In this instance use only a light oil to prevent component seizure.

Although the Buses we are looking at within this book are now up to 50 years old and no longer carry a VW warranty, the performance components that you fit should come with some form of guarantee. To prevent any voiding of this warranty, use the components in the way that the manufacturer or supplier recommends, and always keep receipts for the parts you use. If your modification substantially alters the performance or specification of the Bus, you'll have to notify your insurance company to prevent any problems in the event of a future claim. If the parts suppliers doesn't provide comprehensive fitting instructions, make sure you know how to fit the parts, or talk to other owners who have already done the modification you are considering, and find out how this will alter the performance of your Bus.

Finally, remember to read this book in conjunction with a detailed workshop manual. There are many good manuals available, and each has something to offer in the way of photography, technical specification, and practical advice. Read and re-read the sections on the area of your Bus that you're interested in, and make sure you're familiar with the components before you start tearing the Bus apart. By reading this book alongside a good workshop manual, you will appreciate the type of changes

that are possible to the VW design, and whether they are right for you and your Bus. Don't create a Bus that is dangerous because the parts you are using will only perform correctly if additional components are also fitted. For instance, does the disc brake kit you are considering come with the correct master cylinder, brake lines, brake pads etc. or are they all extras? Will the conversion work with the modifications to the suspension height and type of wheel and tyres you are planning? The Bus should be fun to drive - don't undo the good work that VW put into the design in the first place!

The publisher, author, editors and retailer of this book accept no responsibility for personal injury or mechanical damage that results from using the book, howsoever caused, even if this is through omissions or errors in the text. If this disclaimer is unacceptable to you, please return the pristine book to your retailer who will refund the purchase price.

TOOLS
Whilst it is always possible to hire tools, or borrow them if you belong to a VW club, there is no substitute for having your own set of tools so that you can work on your Bus at any time you choose. Good quality brand-name tools may be an expensive outlay in one go, so be prepared to 'collect' tools over a period of time, and build up your toolbox gradually. Although cheaper tools will appear tempting, they tend to also be poor quality and will not last as long or work as efficiently as the better-known makes, so shop wisely and check out the prices of several dealers before parting with any cash.

There will be certain items that are a must for any toolbox, and these will include a selection of metric

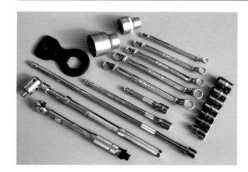

Good quality tools are a necessity for safety and will last longer. Spanners, sockets, a torque wrench and rear axle nut tool are all 'must-have tools'.

spanners (wrenches) in both open-ended (crescent) and ring (box end) form. The most common sizes for a VW Bus include 10mm, 11mm, 13mm, 15mm, 17mm and 19mm, so make sure that these are included in any set you purchase. If you are trying to remove rounded-off nuts, then a set of Metwrinch 4WD double-ended spanners are worth having, as their design allows the internal spanner surface to work entirely on the nut faces, rather than the corners. You'll also need a wide selection of sockets in similar metric sizes, and it's worth having both a 'standard' set, and a 'deep socket' set. The latter being particularly useful to get onto nuts that are difficult to access without a longer reach. Extension bars, 'wobble' bars

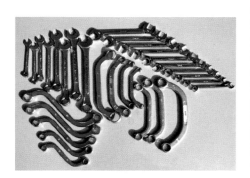

Metric spanners in open ended, ring, offset and Metwrinch designs are all useful tools in your kit.

(designed to allow some movement of the socket at the far end of the bar), joints, and socket drive adaptors (to allow different socket sizes to attach to larger or smaller bars) are also useful additions. You will, of course, need a socket drive, and a ratcheted one that will allow you to turn the socket either way on a nut to loosen or tighten it is recommended.

Other essentials are a set of screwdrivers with different shaft ends (straight or cross-head), and in a selection of sizes and lengths. Allen keys (hex keys) in both metric and imperial sizes are also prerequisites for a Bus toolkit, as are pliers, a selection of drifts, bearing pullers, a bearing removal and installation tool, ball-joint separators (available in several different designs, from the small wind-down type to the larger and

Ball joint separators come in different designs from the wind down type to the more brutal 'pickle fork'

more brutal - but ultimately far more effective - 'pickle fork' type), and both internal and external circlip (snapring) pliers. A nicety is to have a selection of locking-jaw pliers (Mole grips). Their design allows them to self-lock onto an item, and can act as a 'third hand' for you in certain situations. They come in a wide variety of different sizes and jaw designs, such as straight, curved, long-nose, or fitted with paddles (for welding use).

Moving on to more specialised tools, if you're planning to tackle work on the rear brakes of the Bus

it will entail removing the rear axle shaft nut. Vehicles manufactured prior to 1963 use 36mm nuts, and those thereafter 46mm. Whichever design your Bus has, you will need a corresponding sized socket, socket drive bar, and a long extension pole (such as scaffolding tube about 6ft long to increase leverage) to be able to undo these stubborn items. They are tightened to a terrific torque of 217ft/lb

Removing the rear axle nut requires a large 36mm (or 46mm) socket, a basic axle nut tool, or this special Torque-Meister tool for increased leverage.

on the 36mm nuts, and 253ft/lb on the 46mm ones, and require considerable strength to undo and re-tighten. One alternative is to use a special US-made tool called a Torque-Meister. This uses a chromoly steel plate bolted to the brake drum to allow a gear shaft fitted to the 36mm nut at one end and an ordinary torque wrench at the other to multiply the pressure you apply to the wrench and thus release the hub nut. For example, a 30ft/lb torque applied to the wrench produces 270ft/lb of torque at the axle nut. For the tool to work on the 46mm nut, a special socket has to be made utilising the end part of a 46mm socket welded to a flanged 36mm VW axle nut. Whilst it is a special - and expensive - tool for a one-off use, it comes into its own if you regularly work on VWs, as it can also be used to remove the engine flywheel gland nut, which is similarly torqued-up.

To remove the CV joints on your Bus (post '68) you'll also need a special splined tool that fits into the hex-head bolts holding IRS CV joints to their flanges. This usually comes in a fitting to allow it to be used with a $1/2$in socket drive ratchet bar.

Sets of similar hex bits and screwdriver bits are also available to fit into a special socket holder, which attaches to a standard socket drive bar or impact driver. This is particularly helpful when extra turning force is required to loosen stubborn items. Other 'special' tools that can be purchased include brake adjusters (for rapid turning of the 'star' adjusters within a VW brake drum), a brake shoe retaining clip removal and refitting tool, and a bleed nipple spanner. One last 'tool' that is worth a mention is a good quality penetrating and lubricating fluid, such as WD 40. Spray

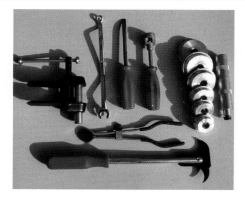

Brake tools include (l-r) a piston return tool, bleed nipple spanner, brake adjuster, shoe retaining clip removal tool, seal refitting tool and below a brake line clip and seal removal tool.

this on seized or frozen components for a few days before attempting removal, and let the components soak thoroughly. Its value cannot be underestimated, and will get you out of a lot of problems with stubborn and rusted VW parts!

Choosing tools is a matter of personal preference, and actual

need. Work on the rear suspension calls for a camber-adjustment protractor to ensure accurate setting and equalisation of both sides of the suspension, but will you use this equipment more than once or twice? If not, then consider renting it. Similarly with welding equipment, it may be cheaper to hire a good set of welding equipment for the day, rather than buying it and leaving it in a corner of your garage unused for most of the time. If you need further information on the capability of certain tools or equipment before you buy or rent, ask the supplier or a qualified mechanic - the advice they give will cost you nothing, but could save an expensive mistake. If you can talk to another Bus owner who has made the same modification that you're considering, so much the better. Learn from their experience, and enjoy yourself as you create the Bus of your dreams!

Chapter 1

Chassis, suspension & brake design

IN THE BEGINNING

The VW Transporter first appeared in Volkswagen blueprints as early as 1948, although full production would not take place for another two years. The vehicle's introduction was born out of a post war necessity for economic and reliable transport, and as a commercial response to competition. The design also heeded

Plattenwagens were crude VW-based transporters used to move components around the VW factory.
(Courtesy Walter Bach)

Front-wheel drive commercial vehicle, the Tempo Matador, used the air-cooled engine from a VW Beetle.

the recommendations of Ben Pon, a Dutch VW importer, who had already recognised a market need beyond the Beetle. Pon had seen the crude vehicles used to transport components around the VW factory (called Plattenwagens) - which were essentially the axles and drivetrain of a wartime Kubelwagen attached to a ladder frame - and quickly appreciated their potential as commercial vehicles. Failing to get street-legal certification

on this design in the Netherlands, due to the location of the driving position at the rear, he nevertheless argued that VW should produce a more refined transporter to meet growing market needs.

His efforts may have been incidental, however, as VW was more concerned with the appearance of

View of the Tempo Matador chassis, steering and drivetrain.

the Tempo Matador forward control vans and trucks from the firm of Vidal und Sohn KG in Hamburg. These lightweight commercial vehicles used an air-cooled Volkswagen engine attached to a ZF gearbox, but located in a forward position within a separate tubular chassis. With the driver and passenger sitting above the front axle line in a forward control position, and within the comfort of an enclosed cab, the front-wheel drive Tempo was launched in 1949, and achieved creditable sales in the commercial sector, stealing a lucrative market from under VW's nose.

The Lieferwagen was the first VW van/panel truck prototype, commissioned from a local garage. (Courtesy Walter Bach)

The Volkswagen factory had certainly considered a van project in the British-run post war years, but since production of the KDF Beetle ('Strength Through Joy' car) fully occupied factory capacity, the first recognisable VW van/panel truck prototype, called the Lieferwagen, didn't appear until 1946, and was commissioned from a local garage at Wolfsburg. This looked very similar to the Beetle shape, but attempted to

VW's first recognisable Transporter – literally a 'box on wheels' – was developed in 1949. (Courtesy Walter Bach)

stretch the KDF body into a delivery vehicle form. However, this limited the internal carrying space, and the unmodified KDF platform chassis couldn't withstand the additional load capacity.

Rather than pursue the idea of a separate body and chassis, the design

The Transporter used a body and chassis welded together to create a lightweight yet immensely strong commercial vehicle. (Courtesy Simon Glen)

was begun again to create a functional 'box on wheels'. It was designed from the outset to offer tremendous load carrying capacity ($^3/_4$ of a metric ton in 162cu ft) by taking the load between the axles, and with a cab-forward driving position so that the driver and passenger's weight would perfectly balance that of the rear-mounted engine and fuel tank behind the rear

axle transmission. The vehicle was built to a lightweight 'aircraft-type' design with the body and chassis welded together. With a wheelbase identical to that of the Beetle, light steering and good vision, the vehicle was designed to feel and drive more like a car than a commercial vehicle. This was to be the key to its worldwide success, as here was a practical vehicle that could be used by all, whether for commerce or for leisure.

From the initial commercial need, the prototype VW Transporter was born. It would go on to capture a 30% market share in the under-one tonne commercial vehicle market a mere four years after its full launch in 1950. With sales in the millions in the years since, it has become one of the most influential vehicle designs in the world.

SPLIT-SCREEN BUS (1950 - 1967)
Chassis

The first unitary construction prototype was based around a subframe incorporating two longitudinal steel chassis rails, welded to front and rear crossmembers, and three transverse chassis rails between the front and rear axles. Outer box members added reinforcement to the basic structure,

Cutaway of Transporter panel van.

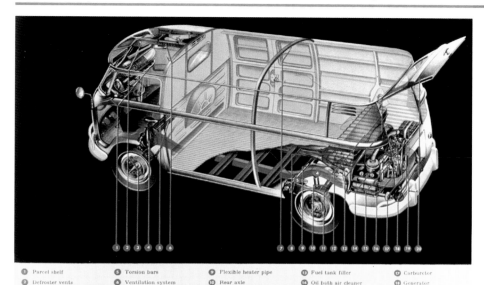

① Parcel shelf	⑤ Torsion bars	⑨ Flexible heater pipe	⑬ Fuel tank filler	⑰ Carburetor
② Defroster vents	⑥ Ventilation system	⑩ Rear axle	⑭ Oil bath air cleaner	⑱ Generator
③ Brake wheel cylinder	⑦ Dome lamp	⑪ Spur reduction gears	⑮ Distributor	⑲ Battery
④ Telescopic shock absorber	⑧ Transmission	⑫ Fuel tank	⑯ Fuel pump	⑳ Rear loading door

Promotional literature shows the structure of the Transporter.

and provided stability to areas such as the vehicle doors and window frames. Body panels, such as the sheet-metal floor and interior walls, were also reinforced by heavy ribbing to prevent susceptibility to flexing.

The design was not a true chassis in the accepted engineering sense as it also relied on this frame to be welded to the body panels, allowing them to strengthen each other and provide torsional rigidity. However, this revolutionary amalgamation of a ladder-frame chassis, welded floorpan

Two longitudinal chassis rails were welded to cross members and transverse chassis rails for stability and strength. (Courtesy Alex Leighton)

sections and body panels, to provide a monocoque, gave the whole structure incredible strength, and was a radical departure from the heavy standalone chassis of most contemporary commercial vehicles and cars.

Since the concept of the VW Transporter was built around a cargo space (and not an available chassis), the design determined that the carrying space lay exactly between the axles, and thus the cargo weight was carried centrally for perfect balance. With the steering situated forward of the front axle, it allowed the front seat occupants to be situated directly above it, matching the rear-mounted engine and drivetrain weight. This consideration of weight distribution within the initial designs of the Transporter chassis and suspension systems ensured that even a well-loaded vehicle handled extremely well on all terrains. The vehicle - weighing approx 2150lb (975kg) - could easily cope with carrying a load of 1632lb (740kg) , making it an ideal delivery vehicle or camper.

Acknowledging its heritage from the Beetle - and meeting requirements to make the Transporter 'feel' like a car - the wheelbase was set at 94.5in (2400mm) (identical to the Beetle), with the turning circle being a modest 33ft (10.1m) on left lock and 35ft (10.7m) on right lock, and the lock-to-lock of the steering wheel a mere 2.8 turns. The chassis of the Split-screen Transporter remained virtually unchanged, apart from additional strengthening in 1955, until the introduction of the Bay-window model in 1968, when the Transporter range was modernised.

Front suspension

Like the Beetle saloon, the design of the suspension system utilised the well proven Porsche-designed torsion bar springing arrangement, front and rear. At the front, an immensely strong torsion bar suspension assembly - made up of two transversely mounted tubes containing leaf torsion bars, mounted one above the other and held in position by steel uprights bolted to the main chassis rails - provided a comfortable ride on all types of road surface. Since the thin leaves, which made up the composite torsion bar, were bolted at their outer ends to trailing arms (and in turn to the hubs), and were also affixed in the centre of the tube to an internal locating block by a dog-tooth screw and lock-nut, the effect was of two torsion bars from each assembly, making four bars in all.

The torsion leaves - initially five in the lower tube and four in the upper tube (later nine each) made of tempered metal - also gave a rising rate springing effect since they resisted the upward motion of the wheels on the ground. The more the suspension was twisted, the higher the spring rating became, providing a smoother ride for the occupants.

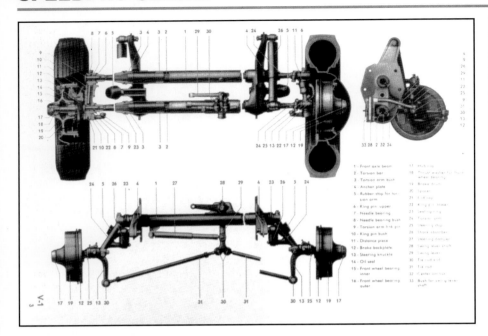

The following labels appear in the diagram legend:

1 - Front axle beam
2 - Torsion bar
3 - Torsion arm bush
4 - Anchor plate
5 - Rubber stop for torsion arm
6 - King pin upper
7 - Needle bearing
8 - Needle bearing bush
9 - Torsion arm link pin
10 - King pin bush
11 - Distance piece
12 - Brake backplate
13 - Steering knuckle
14 - Oil seal
15 - Front wheel bearing inner
16 - Front wheel bearing outer
17 - Hub cap
18 - Thrust washer for front wheel bearing
19 - Brake drum
20 - King pin
21 - Felt ring
22 - King pin lower
23 - Sealing ring
24 - Torsion arm
25 - Steering box
26 - Shock absorber
27 - Steering damper
28 - Swing lever shaft
29 - Swing lever
30 - Tie rod end
31 - Tie rod
32 - Centre steering
33 - Bush for swing lever shaft

The transporter king and linkpin front suspension.

Rising rate torsion bar springing was used to provide suspension akin to that of a car, rather than a commercial vehicle.

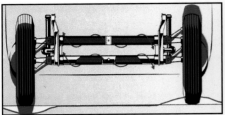

The torsion leaves were fixed in the centre and at each end, giving an effect of two torsion bars from each assembly.

Each of the parallel trailing arms - attached to the outer ends of the torsion leaf stacks by a dog-tooth screw and lock nut - pivoted on bearings housed inside the torsion tubes themselves. The trailing arms were connected to the hubs by adjustable king and linkpins which required regular greasing to keep them lubricated. These durable units provided the pivot for the steering. The horizontally-mounted case-hardened linkpins ran in needle roller bearings, and had helical adjustment grooves on their shanks engaging the pinch bolts. The vertically-mounted upper and lower kingpins were mounted in plain metal bushes, and acted as the steering pivots.

One-piece hubs and brake drums ran on the steering knuckle spindle on ball bearings until 1960, and taper-roller bearings thereafter. Also from the same year, a stabilizer (anti-roll) bar was attached to the lower trailing arms by rubber bushings and retaining clips to help reduce the body roll of the vehicle.

The front suspension uprights of the torsion bar assembly provided the top location for the shock absorbers (dampers), whilst the bottom mounting was at the outer end of the bottom trailing arms. Fitting a solid rubber bump stop between the torsion arms enhanced the telescopic hydraulic dampers. This was changed on later models to upper and lower rubber bump mounts.

Steering gear

With the forward control position of the driver, the steering gear of the Transporter was itself mounted ahead of the front axle and was a ZF type utilizing the worm and peg principle. The inner steering column, attached to the steering wheel at the top, had an integral worm (like a helical groove) machined at the lower end. When turned, the worm engaged a peg (or cam) within the steering box and transmitted the rotary motion via a lever shaft that was splined at the outer end, and onto which was fitted a drop arm. This in turn pushed (or pulled) on a transverse drag link - essentially a rod, ball jointed at either end - connected to a shaped swing lever pivoting on a bracket welded to the lower torsion tube of the front axle. This lever operated two unequal length track rods with ball-jointed ends, and transmitted the steering movement to the steering arms of the stub axle assemblies. The steering box was bolted to a special chassis member by a bracket.

Although seemingly complicated, it was a responsive and efficient system, and could be adjusted and easily maintained. A steering damper was also fitted to models from 1955 onwards, and the steering gearbox itself was changed to a 'drag-free' worm and roller unit in 1961.

Brakes

Hydraulically-operated single-circuit drum brakes were initially used on all four wheels, with the brake drum size of 230mm (on 1200cc models, later 247mm on the 1500cc models) providing a much larger and more effective braking friction area than that of the Beetle. Front brakes were initially of a single-cylinder design, with an integral serrated adjuster. After 1955, however, a second brake cylinder was added. The front brakes utilized a twin leading shoe design to provide maximum braking efficiency at the front of the heavy vehicle, whilst at the rear, a single leading shoe and a trailing shoe were considered adequate. The rear brakes remained with a single cylinder, but with serrated adjusters located separately. The size of the master cylinder, which included a fluid reservoir mounted directly to it, was increased on 1961 - 1967 Transporters from a bore size of 19.05mm to 22mm, and became a tandem operation in 1963 to feed both front and rear brake circuits. A dual circuit system was later introduced as a safety requirement. The handbrake was a conventional cable operated system working on each back drum.

Rear suspension

At the rear of the chassis, the two solid torsion bars (springs) of the rear suspension - fixed at the inner end by splines - were located within each end of a tubular housing, which in turn was positioned transversely in front of the gearbox. With spring plate trailing arms attached to the outer splined ends of the torsion bars and to the swinging half axles of the transaxle, the layout

was unmistakably similar to the durable independent swinging axle design of the Beetle.

Indeed, the gearbox itself was initially a Beetle item, but with the ring gear fitted to the opposite side to allow the use of auxiliary reduction hub gearboxes on the outer ends of the drive shafts - in a fashion similar to the wartime Kubelwagen. These reduction boxes took the strain off the gears in the main case when pulling away from rest. They gave better acceleration to the humble 1131cc engine and also increased ground clearance (by 3in), but would have reversed the vehicle's gears without the ring gear modification.

Since the outboard reduction boxes provided more gears to share the torque multiplication whilst being driven, the loads on the individual gear teeth were reduced - thus ensuring a

Reduction hub gearboxes took the strain off the main gearbox, and gave greater ground clearance for the vehicle. (Courtesy Alex Leighton)

longer working life for the gears. They also had a lower overall gearing, and were made available in a 1.39:1 ratio

Rear suspension was of solid torsion bar type, with a swing axle layout that was strong and durable, but susceptible to adverse camber changes. (Courtesy Malcolm Bobbitt)

for early models, changing to a 1.26:1 ratio on Buses after mid-1963. This higher ratio compensated for the lower final drive ratio in the main gearbox, which was adopted to address the overall 'taller' gearing of the 1500cc engine fitted at this time. Other, more specialised ratios, such as 1.68:1, were also made available, but are not particularly common on Buses outside mainland Europe.

The 'swing axle' design of the rear suspension is more correctly a hybrid between a pure swing axle system and trailing arms. This allows cornering loads to be taken up by the spade and socket universal joint design of the axles at each side of the gearbox. The single trailing arm spring plates that attach to the torsion bar outer ends via splines, also attach to the transaxle outer axle tubes carrying the rear hub and brake assemblies. As the trailing arm spring plates are subjected to force as the rear suspension is raised or compressed the rear hubs (and the wheels and tyres) describe an arc, which creates a high roll centre, as the axle pivots at the transaxle end, and consequently, less desirable handling characteristics.

The design does not allow for any sideways movement to correct such changes in camber, due to the rigid axle tubes, and the end result is a vehicle that displays a twitchiness at the rear in the wet, or over uneven road surfaces. This 'fault' was changed on later models for safety reasons by fitting a four-joint Independent Rear Suspension (IRS).

At the rear of the chassis, two supported forked members, attached to the torsion bar tube, mounted the gearbox. The gearbox was attached at three strategic points. One at the centre of the torsion tube (beneath the 'nose' of the gearbox that provided the coupling for the gear lever

change rod), and the other two on a removable support bolted transversely across the very ends of the forks. Mounting blocks made of rubber-faced steel helped insulate the Bus interior from engine and gearbox vibration, whilst also protecting the gearbox from engine torque.

Attached to the bell-housing end of the gearbox was the Porsche-designed, horizontally-opposed, four-cylinder, air-cooled engine. Initially this was of 1131cc capacity, but was increased to 1192cc in 1953, and then 1493cc in 1963 to gain additional power for Buses destined for the American market.

BAY-WINDOW BUS (1968 - 1979)
Chassis

The design of the revolutionary Transporter was changed from the familiar Split-screen front windscreen style to the Bay-window style for the 1968 model. Besides the obvious change in the appearance of the body, with its curved, one-piece panoramic window, there were many other new developments incorporated to improve the vehicle and keep it commercially competitive in the marketplace. Although VW started the design afresh,

The chassis of the Bay-window Transporter – introduced for the 1968 model year – was totally redeveloped to meet new vehicle safety regulations.
(Courtesy Walter Bach)

the wheelbase remained at 94.5in (2400mm), but the overall body length increased by 4in (160mm) because of the increased front and rear overhangs. With modifications to the chassis and drivetrain design a lowered floor could also be introduced enlarging the usable interior space to 177cu ft, and increasing the payload capacity to one tonne.

The chassis was redeveloped to conform to stricter vehicle legislation, particularly in the US. The front part of the structure now incorporated 'Y'-shaped members on the chassis that would provide additional safety for the front seat occupants in the event of a frontal collision. Coupled with a deformable safety steering column, this type of progressive design thinking was only introduced on other

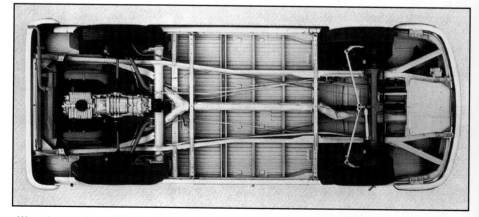

Worm's eye view of the Bay-window chassis and running gear. Revised rear suspension layout is clearly visible. (Courtesy Malcolm Bobbitt)

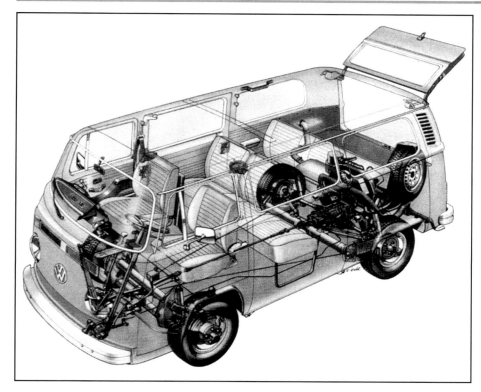

Ghosted view of the Bay-window Bus.

(the transmission now being mounted on a carrier), and the transverse torsion bar tube now formed an integral part of the strength of the chassis, with additional metal supports welded between the tube and the main longitudinal chassis members. The independent 'swing axle' design of rear suspension with outer reduction gearboxes was replaced with the vastly superior IRS (Independent Rear Suspension) using short, solid axles mounted between two constant velocity (CV) joints per side of the gearbox. The inner CV joints were bolted to flanges mounted on each side of the gearbox. The outer two were bolted to similar flanges which formed part of the two short splined axles. These ran in bearings in the hub carriers to which the brake drums were mounted. Additionally, a semi-trailing 'A' arm located the rear hub and wheel instead of the axle tube as before. With the CV joints allowing for angular movement of the axle as the

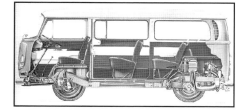

Cutaway of the Bus showing the running gear and drivetrain of the second-generation design.
(Courtesy Walter Bach)

forward-control vans like the Toyota Previa as late as 1987. The chassis had two redesigned longitudinal box sections, front and rear crossmembers, and a series of outriggers supporting the bodywork, welded into a unitary structure for maximum strength.

Rear suspension
At the rear, the Transporter's previous transmission frame forks were removed

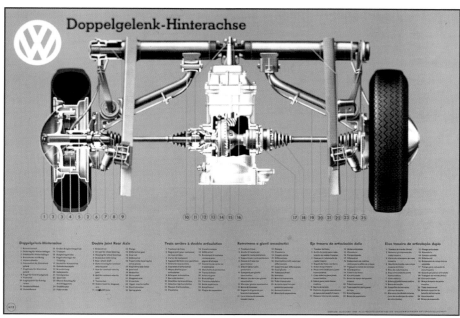

Independent Rear Suspension (IRS) provided vastly improved road holding, and greater durability for the transaxle.

suspension moved up and down, and minimising adverse camber changes, the wheels were much less likely to 'tuck in', and the roadholding became more neutral, and safer.

The design also made the transaxle more durable, since any strains that were previously transmitted directly to the transaxle were now absorbed through the double CV joints of the IRS unit. Lateral forces (side loads), that helped damage a swing axle transmission, were now transmitted to the torsion tube through the diagonal 'A' arms. The adoption of the IRS system also slightly widened the rear track on the new model.

Although this four joint system is popularly known as an IRS, this is something of a misnomer since even the previous design was also an 'independent suspension'. However, IRS has now become the accepted term to describe this design.

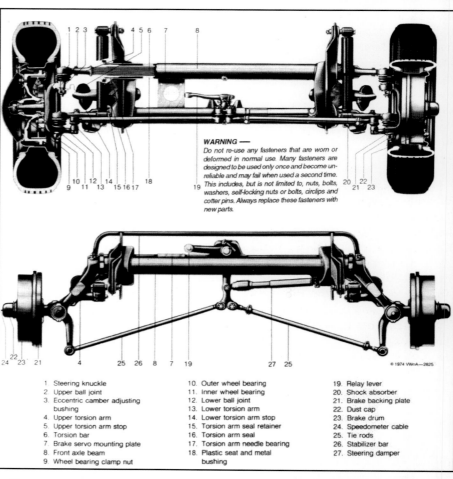

WARNING —
Do not re-use any fasteners that are worn or deformed in normal use. Many fasteners are designed to be used only once and become unreliable and may fail when used a second time. This includes, but is not limited to, nuts, bolts, washers, self-locking nuts or bolts, circlips and cotter pins. Always replace these fasteners with new parts.

1. Steering knuckle	10. Outer wheel bearing	19. Relay lever
2. Upper ball joint	11. Inner wheel bearing	20. Shock absorber
3. Eccentric camber adjusting bushing	12. Lower ball joint	21. Brake backing plate
4. Upper torsion arm	13. Lower torsion arm	22. Dust cap
5. Upper torsion arm stop	14. Lower torsion arm stop	23. Brake drum
6. Torsion bar	15. Torsion arm seal retainer	24. Speedometer cable
7. Brake servo mounting plate	16. Torsion arm seal	25. Tie rods
8. Front axle beam	17. Torsion arm needle bearing	26. Stabilizer bar
9. Wheel bearing clamp nut	18. Plastic seat and metal bushing	27. Steering damper

The revised front suspension of the Bay-window Bus moved away from the king and linkpin design to ball joints.

Close-up of the driveshaft, constant velocity joints and diagonal 'A' arm of the IRS design.

Front suspension & brakes

The front axle was such a robust and well-loved design, that this was the one main component in the redesign that remained largely unaltered. Its only major overhaul was the replacement of the older king and linkpins (which required regular maintenance), with ball joints. Apart from some strengthening and a slight increase in the front track, it remained much as before, and was bolted to the main longitudinal legs of the chassis frame in the same way. Only in 1970 did the front suspension assembly no longer become interchangeable between

models, when the bolt-mountings on the chassis were spaced further apart.

A year later, modern front disc brakes with a brake proportioning valve were introduced. These replaced the former drums though all brakes had been dual-circuit since the introduction of the Bay-window model. This was to compensate for the larger 1700cc engine size introduced in 1971, which would increase to 1800cc, and then to 2-litres by 1975 in a bid to woo new customers.

In 1974, the front disc brakes were further enhanced by the addition of a brake servo unit. With the introduction of disc brakes, the wheel bolt pattern changed to a smaller five-bolt 112mm PCD (Pitch Circle Diameter - the diameter of the circle that passes through the centre of all the wheel stud or bolt holes) - from the original larger five-bolt 205mm. The wheel size itself had already reduced from 16in to 15in in 1955, and then to 14in in 1963.

Later models

Whilst the design of the VW Transporter, in its two former guises, had created a huge niche for itself in the commercial marketplace, others had begun to catch up. VW, therefore, had to re-think the whole future of its Transporter range for the 1980s. The result of VW's redesign was the T3 (or Type 25 as it has become well-known). This 'Wedge-shaped' third-generation Transporter was a very different beast from those that had gone before, with

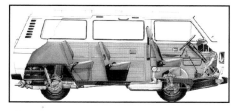

Side-view cutaway of the third-generation (T3) Bus, popularly known as the 'Type 25' or 'Wedge' design. (Courtesy Walter Bach)

a wholly new chassis providing a larger load capacity, and a lower floor.

Whilst construction of the unitized body to a reinforced chassis remained similar in principle - with two longitudinal chassis members, supporting crossmembers and outriggers welded to the floor panels - just about everything else was different, including the suspension. The robust torsion bar suspensions, front and rear, finally gave way to more modern (and cheaper to produce) progressive coil springs, double wishbones, an

Ghosted view of the revised Transporter, with larger load capacity, lower floor, and revised suspension layouts. (Courtesy Walter Bach)

anti-roll bar at the front, and coil springs and trailing arms at the rear. The adoption of this layout allowed a significantly more spacious interior and saved weight, which, with the more aerodynamic design of the body, were all positive selling points.

Rack and pinion steering was also introduced to give a lighter and more responsive feel. The improved weight distribution (51% on the front axle and 49% at the rear), helped reduce body roll and the tendency of previous Transporters to oversteer, thus improving handling.

Progressive coil spring design of the T3 front suspension allowed more interior space, cheaper manufacture, and weight saving. (Courtesy Simon Glen)

Such improvements paved the way for a new chapter in the history and development of the VW range but, for many enthusiasts, the phasing out of the air-cooled engines in 1982 - 1983 was the end of an era.

View of the revised rear suspension layout, with coil springs and trailing arms, leaving little of the earlier designs remaining.

Later versions of VW transporters have continued since 1991 with the T4, which sported a front-mounted transverse engine arrangement, front-wheel drive and a range of water-cooled engines in both petrol and diesel versions. The T4 and the Sharan MPV may be the future of VW's commercial and recreational range of vehicles but it's the older vehicles that still attract the most loyal following amongst VW enthusiasts.

Aftermarket suppliers

Over the last few years there has been a marked rise in the popularity of the Split-screen and Bay-window Buses, and it's no surprise, therefore, that aftermarket suppliers have followed this trend by developing specialist parts specifically for these models. Many of these concentrate on the supply of hard-to-find body panels, mechanical repair components, or interior restoration parts. However, there are a growing number of manufacturers and suppliers of performance components for Bus suspensions and brakes, and it's these that we'll be specifically covering in this book. Already there are major suppliers of parts from the US, the UK, Germany and Australia, and the market is still growing.

With the increased availability of performance components in so many parts of the world, devotees of the classic VW Buses can improve their Transporter's underpinnings to make it drive, handle and stop more like a modern vehicle. How you choose and use these components or how you want your Bus to look and feel, of course, is entirely up to you. You'll no doubt have your own ideas on what's right, but the information in this book will at least offer some choices. The details and photos included here are shown to illustrate the diversity of what's available through aftermarket parts suppliers, but it should by no means be considered definitive. New parts, and new suppliers, are appearing on a regular basis, so who knows what the future will hold?

Talk to other Bus owners, who may have performed the same modifications, to get a true feel of what is involved, in terms of the end result, and the inevitable pitfalls and costs incurred in making the conversions. Joining a club for VW Buses is a great way to meet other like-minded enthusiasts, and to share information and advice. Also talk to the suppliers about their products, and compare parts and prices. Bus equipment tends to be more expensive than the equivalent components for, say, a VW Beetle, and that's the nature of the beast. It is a bigger vehicle and parts for it, by their very nature, are more substantial and expensive.

Whilst there is a plethora of VW Bus repair and workshop guides available, the content of this book has been devoted solely to upgrading the performance of the suspension and brake systems. Whatever your involvement with VW Buses - from home mechanic to professional repair workshop - there'll certainly be something of interest within these pages ...

Chapter 2

Front suspension & brakes

The underside of a fully restored 1963 Split-screen Bus. The front suspension is a very strong unit, with steering pivots provided by king and linkpins. (Courtesy Alex Leighton)

The front suspension fitted to a VW Bus is, by its very nature, an incredibly strong unit. It has to be, as it has almost one ton of weight riding on it. Since it is such a robust design it's tempting to think that parts will not easily wear out. However, like all things mechanical, this isn't the case and you'll need to routinely check items for wear and excessive play. This is particularly true of the earlier king and linkpin style front suspension unit fitted to Split-screen Buses, so we will start by looking at that design.

KING & LINKPIN FRONT SUSPENSION

All VW Buses produced up until July 1967 used a king and linkpin front suspension design. This features steering knuckles with stub axles swivelled on upper and lower kingpins, within kingpin carriers. The knuckles are turned by the action of ball-jointed track rods operated by a swing lever shaft pivoted at a mounting point on the lower torsion bar tube. This, in turn, is operated by a drag link that attaches, at the forward end, to a pitman arm. This is turned by the action of the steering gearbox and ultimately the vehicle steering wheel.

Kingpin carrier - that forms part of the steering knuckle - is seen behind the front drum brakes. Two linkpins attach the carrier to the trailing arms. (Courtesy Alex Leighton)

Replacement parts such as the linkpins, roller bearings and bushes are readily available when rebuilding the front suspension.

The kingpin carriers locate the road wheel hubs and brakes. These are attached to the trailing arms, and thus the torsion bars, by horizontally-mounted, case-hardened linkpins that run in roller bearings located within the carriers. The outer ends of the linkpins are located by a flange (and covered with a dust cap), whilst the inner ends have squared sections that allow spanner adjustment. The linkpins are secured into the split eye section of the trailing arms with pinch bolts - though the lower pinch bolts also require the removal of cotter pins first before removal.

The linkpins have helical grooves cut into their shanks (which engage the pinch bolts of the trailing arms) so that turning the pin adjusts end float as it rotates. This adjustment, together with spacing shims of different thicknesses that sit each side of the linkpin roller bearing in the carrier, sets the suspension geometry. The upper and lower kingpins run in bushes, which are press fitted into the respective parts of the carrier. These provide the pivot on which the steering knuckle rotates. Lubrication of the internal components is facilitated by three grease nipples on each assembly. Providing components are well maintained and regularly lubricated, the system is very durable. However, the superior roadholding and easy maintenance of ball-joints led to the design being changed for the post 1968 Bus suspension.

Checking the king & linkpin suspension for wear

Before we look to modify anything, here is a quick way to test for problems with the main items in the early Bus king and linkpin front suspension and steering design. Firstly, jack up the front of your Bus, and rest it securely on strong axle stands. Holding the top and bottom of the tyre on one side,

Steering swing lever arm rotates on a centre pin located in a mount welded to the lower torsion bar tube. This can be replaced if worn.

rock it back and forth to test for play in the kingpins. Do the same on the other side. If there's any movement, it indicates wear and the pins will have to be replaced.

Moving to the central mount affixed to the front side of the lower axle beam that houses the centre pin and its bushes, place your hand on the top of the swing lever arm that swivels on this pin. Then have a friend turn the Bus steering wheel back and forth. If you feel the arm moving up and down before it begins to turn, then the pin and the bushes need to be replaced. These come in a complete kit ready made for this work, but remember that on Buses up to 1967, the new bushing will have to be reamed to size.

The bushes have spiral-shaped grooves, which start at one end of the bush, and these should face towards the central grease nipple. The bottom bushing must be pressed in flush to the bearing tube, whilst the top bushing should still project 1.4mm - 1.7mm (0.04in - 0.06in). The spring washer, that sits between the top of the shaft and the swing lever, should

Bus steering gearbox, drag link, track rod ball joints and steering damper should all be checked for wear.

If it isn't, it can be adjusted to take up excessive play via an adjusting screw. The steering must not stick at any point during rotation or it won't allow the wheels to return to the 'straight ahead' position after cornering.

If you do replace the steering gearbox, also think of renewing the bronze steering column bushing that fits within the upper part of the column, under the steering wheel, as wear here can also affect the feel of the steering. New bushes for different year Buses are available from companies such as Bluebird Customs in the UK.

REPLACING THE KING & LINKPINS

Overhauling the king and linkpins is the first way to improve the handling of the early Buses. It also provides an opportunity to exchange the steering knuckles for a later, or modified, version that allows a drop in the suspension ride height, or the fitting of disc brakes.

Removing the front hubs to replace the king and linkpins doesn't require the removal of the complete front axle beam. Begin by loosening the wheel nuts, then raise the front of the Bus up on a jack and place it firmly on axle stands. Since the axle won't be removed, place the axle stands under the lower torsion bar tube, as this is a strong point on the Bus. With the road wheels removed, you will see the whole hub and suspension assemblies.

Firstly detach the speedometer drive cable from the nearside hub by removing the small split pin holding the squared end. Then pull the cable back through the hub. The central brake drum grease cap must be pulled off, before the drum itself can be withdrawn. The brake shoes will also require slackening off by turning the brake 'star' adjusters through the hole in the drum with an adjusting tool, or

be sufficiently tensioned to prevent the shaft from rattling when the Bus is moving. A compression of 0.6mm - 0.8mm gives a washer tension of 264lb - 308lb/140kg and prevents this noise.

Also check the drag link and the steering gearbox itself. The drag link is a long rod that goes between the centre pin-mounted swing lever and the pitman arm on the steering box, and it has two track rod ends that are susceptible to wear. With a friend turning the steering wheel, place your hand over each end, in turn, and feel if the ends move within their locating eyes before they push or pull the swing lever. If they do, they're worn and must be replaced.

Finally, the steering gearbox itself can cause problems. A lot of play in the steering, however, doesn't necessarily mean that the box is at fault. Check it by having the steering turned slowly by a friend whilst you

look at the shaft that comes out of the side of the box (and to which the pitman arm attaches). If it moves sideways, before it begins to rotate, it's faulty and will have to be exchanged.

The bronze steering column bushing that fits in the upper part of the column can be replaced to give a precise feel to the steering.

Front brake drums for Buses differ in design depending on the year. Left is 1955 - 1963 drum, whilst right is 1964 - 1967. (Courtesy Custom & Speed Parts)

a screwdriver, to allow the drum to pull free. The whole brake assembly is then accessible, and the shoes and retaining springs can be checked prior to removal.

The 1200cc Buses use 230mm diameter front brake drums, and shoes with a lining width of 50mm, which must not exceed a wear limit of 2.5mm. 1500cc Buses use a 250mm diameter brake drum and shoes measuring 55mm. These should be replaced upon reassembly if wear is excessive. The brake hose that feeds the upper cylinder attaches to a metal bracket fixed on the steering knuckle. The bracket is released by removing the grease nipple that holds it.

The design of the front wheel brakes are of the Duplex type with two leading shoes and two cylinders per wheel connected by a pipe. Undoing any part of the hydraulic system means that the brakes will have to be bled later. The brake hose and the wheel cylinders will have to be removed, since the latter also locate the drum backplate to the knuckle, by the two top and two bottom bolts.

With the backplate removed, the whole steering assembly is accessible.

On each side of the Bus, the outer ball joint of the track rod, that locates and turns the steering arms, must be released. You can choose between different types of ball joint separators for this task. However, if you damage the rubber sleeve of the joint it will have to be replaced or the joint will have a shortened life. Don't hammer on the threaded end of the ball joint pin to release it, but use an extractor. There are several designs on the market from a wind down type to a more brutal 'pickle fork' design.

Now remove the cotterpin from the pinch bolt of the lower torsion arm, and remove the upper and lower pinch bolts. Once freed, the linkpins can be gently tapped out. Alternate between them, until the whole stub axle (knuckle) is free and can be moved to a bench for disassembly. Although the linkpin dust caps can be removed, make a note of the arrangement and the quantity of shims as they are drawn off the linkpins. There should be eight per pin, plus the retainer and rubber seals. Note that from chassis 1 144 303, the diameter of the linkpins was increased from 20mm to 22mm, and the sealing rings, washers and caps

were modified to eliminate wear on the end faces of the torsion arms.

Always order new parts by quoting the chassis number of your Bus, and always replace bushings and needle rollers in sets. The linkpins can be pushed out, the bearings pressed out, and the cleaned parts then inspected for wear. Look for pits in the pins and the outer race and rollers of the bearing. A new kit of parts is available from many aftermarket suppliers. When installing new needle bearings into the upper and lower kingpins ensure that they don't protrude into the recesses that accommodate the shims and that they are a tight press fit. If not, this indicates that the kingpins also need renewal.

The upper kingpin can be extracted from the carrier, with a puller, once the angled nipple has been removed from the top part of the carrier, and the central stop screw has also been withdrawn. The central metal spacer (between the upper and lower kingpin carriers), will then be released, pushed out, and the lower kingpin can then be removed. Inspect the kingpins and their bushes for wear. Apart from these, you may have to replace the thrust washers and seals, which normally come in the overhaul kit. Both kingpin bushes will have to be pressed from the carriers, and the bottom one is accessible once the bottom sealing cap is removed. New bushes must be pressed in, with their faces flush to the stub axle eyes, before both are reamed to size the bushes to a bore of 0.8677in - 0.8699in (22.041mm - 22.020mm). The bushes should be free from any scoring before the kingpins are inserted, and it should be possible to turn the pins, by hand, without any perceptible play.

Once the end cap is refitted, the assembly of the steering knuckle is a reversal of the disassembly process.

Upper kingpin is shown on the left; lower unit is on the right.
(Courtesy Custom & Speed Parts)

Start with the lower kingpin and make sure that the thrust washer (without rubber seal) gives the central spacer an end play of no greater than 0.006in. An oversize spacer is available to correct any play here. Lightly grease the thrust washers and rubber seals before installing them, and use a lever to compress the bottom seal until it's possible to insert the spacer. Re-check that the lower kingpin is free enough to be turned by hand, as it must not bind up in operation. Fit the upper thrust washer and seal, then press the upper kingpin into place with the surfaces greased.

The kingpins must align correctly with each other to give precise movement, so work slowly and carefully. With the rubber seals seated into position, fit the stop screw with its head to the rear, and tighten the nut. Due to the tolerances in the steering lock, three different head sizes are used, so always use the original

(or a similarly sized), stop screw. Finally, check both pins for freedom of movement - you should be able to turn them by hand. If all's well, refit the grease nipple into the top kingpin.

If this all sounds like too much work, then it's possible to buy exchange reconditioned kingpin spindles from companies like Wolfgang International in the US. These spindles have the kingpins replaced, and are ready to bolt back on to your Bus. The next step is to offer the rebuilt knuckle up to the ends of the torsion arm eyes.

You should also check the faces of the eyes for wear or scoring, and the offset of the torsion arm eyes. You can measure the displacement of the lower eye by placing a straight edge between top and bottom eyes. The offset should be 0.276in (7mm), with a tolerance of +/- 0.079in (1.5mm). The offset can be adjusted by inserting the thin metal shims (removed during disassembly) at either side of the upper

and lower linkpins, with a total of eight shims per pin. Each measures 0.026in (0.5mm), and a full table detailing the possible arrangements of these shims is contained within any good VW Bus workshop manual.

This offset is necessary to give the correct kingpin inclination (part of the suspension geometry, which together with wheel camber, gives uniform loading of the wheel bearings, minimises road shocks transmitted to the steering, and returns the wheels to the straight ahead position after cornering). If the offset exceeds the tolerance that can be taken up with the shims, then the torsion arms will need to be replaced.

Lubricate the new link pin bushes, shims and the case-hardened linkpins. Refit them to the torsion arms, adding the pinch bolts to the torsion arms to locate them. The linkpins should be turned to the point where slight resistance is felt, and there is no sideplay to the torsion arms, before the pinch bolts are fully tightened. The lower bolts will need to be secured with cotterpins.

One final modification that can be considered prior to the brake backplates, brake assembly and drums being refitted, is the addition of stronger urethane 'snub' cones to replace the stock rubber items that sit between the trailing arms. The pre-1963 type suspension stops are currently only available from Sway-A-Way, and are the same design as those available for early Beetles. They simply push on to the metal mount and are a good replacement for older items that are generally cracked and ineffective on older Buses. Later model Buses use a larger rubber mount (1964 - 1967), or upper and lower bump stops (post 1968) but these can, of course, be replaced for new items if required.

Once the hub assembly is rebuilt,

Sway-A-Way urethane snub cones (foreground) are available for early suspensions. Rubber bump stops in the background are for 1964 - 1967 models (left), and post '68 models (right).

the brake hoses must be reconnected and the brakes bled and adjusted. Finally, the front wheel camber and toe in should be adjusted at a tyre shop to prevent any uneven tyre wear.

You may wish to change the original flexible brake lines for superior performance stainless steel braided items, or teflon-coated ones, from suppliers such as Bluebird Customs. These not only look better, but are more resistant to any 'bulging' from the 1200psi of the brake fluid when under pressure in the pipes, which could lead to a loss of brake performance.

LOWERED & DISC BRAKE SPINDLES

It's easy to think that the king and linkpin style of front suspension has little to offer in the way of high performance, but that simply isn't so. All Bus front suspensions can be modified, and although we'll look at how to remove and lower front beams

in a separate section, let's find out what is possible with the stock beam remaining in situ.

DROPPED SPINDLES

Initially, those modifying king and linkpin spindles to lower them simply cut the spindles from the stub axle, handed them left to right, and welded them back on in a raised position. Inevitably, the welding produced too much carbon, on what was originally a cast metal item, and couldn't support the weight of the front of the Bus (about 1 ton rides on these components).

The resulting failures led to some different thinking. Lowered spindles are now available in the US, from Wolfgang International, and suppliers in France. They are cast items that are sold in pairs on an exchange basis for your original parts. They come as complete steering knuckles, with new kingpins ready installed, and allow a

$3\frac{1}{2}$in drop, but retain a comfortable suspension ride. Since adding these spindles alters the relationship of the track rods to the front chassis frame, the track rod ends need to be fitted to the pitman arm, from underneath, to allow additional clearance. The eyes of each arm have to be re-drilled, and track rod ends from a 1968-1979 Bus used instead (part number 211 405 801F). The result is a lowered Bus, but caster will be changed.

Since caster (the amount that the top of the kingpin is inclined towards the rear of the vehicle) is very important in keeping the wheels in a straight ahead position when driving, and to prevent wandering, ideally this should be corrected. Unlike a Beetle, where caster shims can be used behind the front axle to realign the geometry, the Bus has no such facility. The only option is to consider re-drilling the front axle mounting holes to incline the camber and compensate for the lowered spindles. Most owners probably won't want to tackle such an operation to restore camber, and although lowering the Bus is achieved it's at the expense of steering geometry.

DISC BRAKE SPINDLES & MASTER CYLINDERS

If you're planning to overhaul the king and linkpins on your Bus, it's also a good time to consider a move to disc brakes. German VW performance specialists, Custom & Speed Parts, supply Brazilian stub axles that will not only fit the early Bus suspension, but they accept disc brakes too. The stub axles aren't lowered, but they are forged, and have an additional section of material, that provides the mounting points, on to which the caliper is bolted. If these are fitted to a lowered Bus, then the pitman arm eyes will need to be re-drilled so that

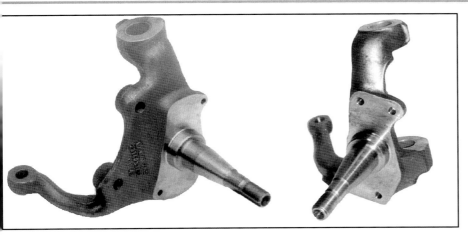

Brazilian VW king and linkpin spindles accept disc brakes (left), and replace drum brake original (right). (Courtesy Custom & Speed Parts)

they'll accept the larger Bay-window ball-jointed track rod ends mounted from underneath.

Rossini performance disc brake can be fitted to early Buses once stub axles are swapped. (Courtesy Paul Knight)

These spindles will then accept 1973 - 1979 Bus hubs, discs (either stock VW items, or grooved and cross-drilled items such as Rossini performance discs) and calipers. This means the wheel bolt pattern on the discs will be 5 x 112mm. By using adaptors such as the billet items supplied by Machine 7, Bluebird

Customs, or Harry Harpic's (all in the UK), these can be changed to the Porsche pattern of 5 x 130mm if you wish to use Porsche-pattern wheels on the Bus.

As with any disc brake conversion to an early Bus, the brake master cylinder will also have to be changed. Custom & Speed Parts, and Wolfgang International in the US, sell a master cylinder adapter kit that allows you to use a dual-circuit 1971 - 1979 Bus master cylinder on the pre-1966 Buses. It also allows those with 1967

Buses to replace the hard-to-find and expensive master cylinder with the later item. You'll also need the 1967-only Bus brake fluid reservoir, or one from a VW Golf (Rabbit), which forms a push fit into the seals in the master cylinder. When installing these reservoirs, put the filling cap end closest to the piston end of the master cylinder, so that you can still refill the reservoir through the removable plate in the Bus cab floor.

For pre-dual circuit brake Buses, you'll also need to source a brass T-fitting and a short metal brake line (which can easily be made up), so that you can replumb the front brake circuits, like those fitted to a 1967 Bus. The metal spacer provided in the kit allows the master cylinder to be positioned further from its mounting bracket, making the push rod far easier to adjust. Check with the adaptor kit supplier whether any modifications are required to the master cylinder actuating push rod, or the bracket it screws into, as some adjustment may be necessary. When fitted, ensure that all the new runs of the metal brake lines are positioned away from moving cables or linkages to prevent any possibility of damage.

Porsche-pattern wheels can be adapted to the disc brakes on a modified Bus, for a custom-look. (Courtesy Custom & Speed Parts)

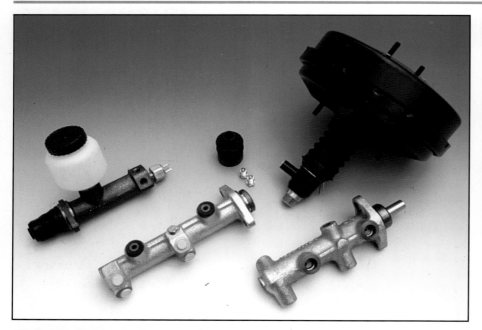

Single-circuit master cylinder (pre-'66) must be changed for later dual-circuit type during a disc brake conversion. The picture shows single-circuit cylinder at rear, and dual-circuit at front. Centre model is a servo-assisted type cylinder.

Servo-assisted brakes fitted to Kruizinwagon T2. Note lowering adjusters in front torsion tubes, and heavy-duty anti-roll bar. (Courtesy Simon Glen)

As a final option, when moving to disc brakes and dual-circuit braking, you can add a brake servo. The vacuum-powered brake servo was offered on 1971 and later Bay-window Buses models with disc brakes. It's a 'fail safe' system - meaning that even if it were to fail, the foot brake can still

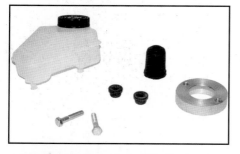

Master cylinder adapter kit allows use of dual-circuit cylinder in early Buses. (Courtesy Custom & Speed Parts)

be applied. It was designed to reduce the pedal pressure required to operate the brakes. It works by allowing the pressure difference between the vacuum in the engine intake manifold and normal atmospheric pressure to move a large diaphragm within the servo unit, which provides an additional force to the master cylinder pushrod. A hose connects the servo to the engine intake manifold via a one way, non-return valve. This enables a low pressure vacuum to operate the servo but cannot blow pressure in the opposite direction if the vehicle backfires, for instance.

Fitting a servo is a very specialised job, since the positioning of the servo unit - which has a special master cylinder attached to it and is located in a different position to a standard dual-circuit master cylinder - requires operation by a connecting rod between the servo and the pedal lever. Attempting this conversion should not be considered unless you're familiar with these systems. Nevertheless, servo assisting the brake system on

a disc (or drum) braked Split-screen (or Bay-window) Bus is a worthwhile modification for a vehicle that sees a lot of daily driving.

DISC BRAKE CONVERSIONS

There are plenty of options now available to owners looking to convert their Split-screen Buses to disc brakes. The first of these is a front disc brake conversion kit by Wolfgang International. It fits the king and linkpin front stub axles, and accepts the discs and calipers from a later 1973 - 1979 Bay-window Bus. The kit comes with special hubs and bearings that fit to the original spindle, 'C' shaped caliper brackets and bolts, seals, and lock tabs. The new hubs effectively replace the complete drum brake assemblies, and the special brackets provide mounts for the calipers. If the Bus, to which they are being fitted, is pre-1966 then the master cylinder will also need to be changed for the dual-circuit disc brake version. The suppliers also recommend using a 15in wheel to allow sufficient clearance for the calipers and brackets.

Kits that use the same basic

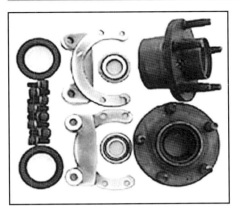

Wolfgang International front disc brake kit accepts discs and calipers from a later 1973-79 Bay-window Bus. (Courtesy Wolfgang International)

Sherman's disc brake kit comes in stock 5 x 205mm PCD wheel bolt fitting. (Courtesy Simon Glen)

principle, but include virtually all new parts (except the original stub axle onto which they fit), are offered by companies such as Neal in the US, Shermans Volks Conversions in Australia, and Custom & Speed Parts in Germany.

The Neal kit uses Willwood calipers (a well-known race-engineered brand of brake caliper), and fits on to the king and linkpin stub axle with shaped metal brackets. They use a disc featuring an 'original look' 5 x 205mm

PCD (Pitch Circle Diameter), but with wheel studs.

Those available from Shermans are similar, but retain wheel bolts - also in a 5 x 205mm PCD. Shermans also sell a similar kit to convert early drum brake Bay-window Buses to vented discs in a 5 x 112mm PCD.

CSP disc brake kit
The Custom & Speed Parts is a supremely well-engineered kit, and is available in different forms to fit not only the 1955 - 1963 and 1964 - 1967 Bus models, but the later Bay-window models 1968 - 1970. The kit consists of CNC-machined caliper brackets,

Neal disc brake conversion kit uses Willwood calipers. Spax coil-over shock absorbers also improve the ride. (Courtesy Volksworld)

Sherman's kit to convert early drum brake Bay-window Buses to vented disc brakes. (Courtesy Simon Glen)

Custom & Speed Parts disc brake kit comes in different forms to fit either 1955 - 1963 or 1964 - 1967 or 1968-1970 Bus models. (Courtesy Custom & Speed Parts)

Creative Engineering cross-drilled discs are available in different PCDs to fit the CSP brake kit.
(Courtesy Creative Engineering)

CNC-machined caliper brackets, Vauxhall/Opel calipers and alloy hubs are all parts of the superbly engineered CSP kit. (Courtesy Custom & Speed Parts)

Vauxhall/Opel calipers (taking easily available replacement disc pads), the disc brake backplates, and alloy hubs with M12 x 1.5mm wheel studs already installed, and bolted to the brake disc itself. All the mounting hardware, bearings, nuts and washers are also included, except the outer wheel bearing adjusting nut and bearing washer from the original drum brake set up.

The beauty of this system is that - since the alloy hub is bolted to the disc rotor - either part can be exchanged or replaced later. Creative Engineering produce both cross-drilled discs and hubs in different PCDs to fit this system. This is advantageous if you're thinking of changing the style of your wheels later on. With all disc conversions you must use the disc brake master cylinder. If you retain the drum brake master cylinder the residual valve (designed to keep brake pressure in the system) will continually add a braking pressure to your discs. This can overheat the discs, and will inevitably cause faster pad wear.

The CSP disc brake kit is very straightforward to fit. The original drum brake system must be stripped down to the spindles, and the hydraulic system will have to be disconnected. The new disc brake caliper bracket must be mounted to the drum brake spindle with the high tensile bolts supplied in the kit. The mounting surface, where the caliper bracket has to be mounted, will need cleaning to remove any loose rust or dirt before bolting down the new bracket. It is important to get the two surfaces flush together.

The whole brake system will work (or fail) based on the mounting of the caliper bracket. The M10 x 20 bolts should have the threads and heads oiled as they are wound in to prevent friction, and they should be torqued to 54ft/lb (73Nm). If you are planning on painting (or coating) your spindles, then the brackets should be mounted first, otherwise the layer of paint between the spindle and the bracket will cause problems with the brake's performance. The bracket must always allow the caliper to be mounted behind the spindle, though the mountings make it appear that it could be positioned either in front or behind the spindle.

The stainless steel dust covers have two purposes. They keep the backs of the discs free from stone damage, and they also guide cooling air to the discs to prevent overheating and distortion. They are mounted with three M6 x 10 hex bolts. The alloy hubs are pre-assembled by CSP, as are the wheel bearings, and they are bench tested for trueness prior to being sold. The disc bolts should not be loosened, as they are part of this testing. The disc bolts should only be changed when the disc is replaced, and they will then have to be tested again for trueness.

Installing the hub/disc is then a case of fitting the rear wheel bearing into the pre-installed race, and adding the rear seal, before slipping it onto the stub axle. The outer bearing must then be fitted, together with the bearing washer and adjusting nut, which must be finally secured before adding the outer grease cap. The speedometer cable can be re-installed, and the squared section run through the hole in the nearside grease cap, and secured with a circlip.

Degrease the disc, then fit the caliper around it, with the bleed nipple at the top. The two M12 x 40 high tensile bolts can then be lightly oiled and added, not forgetting the shims between the caliper and bracket (1964 - 1967 and 1968 - 1970 only). The caliper bolts should be torqued to 58ft/lb (78Nm), and finally, the brake hoses can be re-attached using an adapter and copper sealing ring supplied in the kit. The whole brake system must then be bled to remove

any air that's entered. The CSP disc brake conversion is certainly an impressive kit to look at, and its performance is no less stunning.

PORSCHE DISC BRAKES

Other brake upgrades include the fitting of Porsche 924/944 ventilated front discs to improve braking, and which also allows the use of Porsche pattern 5 x 130mm PCD wheels for a neat, custom touch. Post '72 Bay-window Bus spindles use the same front wheel bearings as the early Porsche 944s, though they are spaced 10mm further apart on the 944. By machining two spacers of 5mm for each side, which are then pressed into the Porsche hubs (the part the disc bolts to), the bearings can be made to sit in the correct position on the Bus stub axles. This allows the hubs and discs to fit straight on.

Wheels with a 65mm offset (such as 16 x 7.5in Porsche 928 wheels) are then required to clear the 4-piston Brembo calipers, which must be attached to the stub axle with a specially machined mounting bracket. Even early Porsche 911 Turbo front hubs have the same bearing spacing as the Porsche 944. To these can be added either the Turbo discs, or the 11in (282mm) diameter, $1\frac{1}{2}$in thick vented and cross-drilled discs from a Porsche 930!

If Porsche conversions are not on your agenda, despite them offering serious performance braking, how about a 13in vented cross-drilled disc suitable for mounting a 16in or 17in alloy wheel from Kruizinwagon in Australia, or vented discs with 4-piston calipers for Split-window Buses from Custom & Speed Parts? Proving again the versatility and the ability to interchange VW components, Kruizinwagon have also fitted VW T3 (Transporter) front discs and calipers to

Kruizinwagon-modified Bay-window Bus with 1971 - 1979 front stub axles and T3 calipers and discs fitted with modification and machining. (Courtesy Simon Glen)

the earlier designs of Bus ... Anything, it seems, is possible.

REMOVING & MODIFYING THE FRONT SUSPENSION

So far, we've looked at conversions

17in alloy wheels and 40 series tyres complement the modified brakes and suspension on Indian Automotive's 2-litre powered Bay-window Bus. (Courtesy Simon Glen)

Porsche 944 ventilated front discs and calipers fitted to the front of a Bay-window Bus for serious stopping power. (Courtesy BBT)

where the complete front suspension has remained in the Bus whilst work has been carried out. In this next section, we will be removing the whole front suspension. This, in itself, is quite a big job so plan to make all the modifications you want whilst the suspension is removed. You'll also need a second person to help you, as the assembly is no featherweight!

There are two basic reasons for taking the front suspension out of the Bus. The first is that the torsion bar tubes or upright shock absorber mounts have corroded and need repairs or replacing. The second is that it is going to be modified in some way. There are plenty of ways to modify the suspension, and we will look at some of the best to see how you can give your Bus a performance make-over.

The example illustrated in the picture sequence is from a Bay-window Bus, but the principle is fundamentally the same for all the T1 and T2 models. You may even consider removing the complete ball joint front suspension from a 1968 - 1969 Bay-window Bus to fit into your earlier Split-screen Bus. This transplant can be done since the chassis sidemember mounting points, for the front suspension uprights, are the same on these models as the earlier king and linkpin design. The advantage is that - having ball-jointed front-steering knuckles - the drum brake components from the stub axle outwards can be removed, and changed, for the disc brake components from a post-1971 Bay-window Bus (the whole suspension from the disc brake models can't be used as the bolt mountings on the chassis were spaced further apart). It's another example of the ability to swop parts on the VW model range.

If you go down this route, and are looking for added performance, the stock VW discs can be swapped for

Lowered ball joint front suspension from a 1968 - 1969 Bay-window Bus fitted to an earlier Split-screen Bus. (Courtesy Paul Utting)

Disc brakes can be transplanted on to any ball-jointed Bus front suspension once the steering knuckles have been changed.

performance cross-drilled and grooved discs made by Rossini Performance Products, and supplied by Car Parts Direct in the UK. These help dissipate heat better on the heavy Bus, as well as looking good! Add some Ferodo Premier brake pads to enhance the stopping power, and ensure that they have the edges chamfered to prevent them squealing on the disc grooves.

Since the whole front suspension will be removed as a complete unit,

When fitting discs, or overhauling a disc brake setup, always use new pads, anti-squeal shims and spreader plates. Check caliper piston function on old calipers, or use new ones.

Rossini cross-drilled and grooved performance discs are available in a Bay-window Bus fitting. (Courtesy Paul Knight)

Underneath the front of the Bus, remove the front metal undertray that covers the clutch and accelerator cables, and the master cylinder. (Courtesy Richard Foks)

make sure the Bus is supported on axle stands that are positioned correctly under the chassis - not under the axle itself - and that the wheels are chocked at the back. This prevents any possible movement since, on the early Buses, the handbrake cables have to be removed.

Removing the front suspension

Begin the strip down process by taking out the rubber mats on the floor of the cab. Then remove the gear lever, noting the way the lockout plate fits underneath it. Moving underneath the front of the Bus, remove the

front metal undertray, which protects the cable linkages for the clutch, accelerator and handbrake equalizer bar (on 1972 and later Transporters), as well as the master cylinder. All the linkages must be disconnected, and pulled clear of the front suspension, with the exception of the accelerator cable on early Buses, which runs above the axle.

The clevis (pivot) pin connecting

the clutch can be awkward to take out, but will be helped by slackening or releasing the clutch cable from the operating lever on the transmission case. The pivot pin is prone to wearing in the lever arm on early models, and can be difficult to withdraw. If it is worn it should be replaced on reassembly, as should the bushing in the arm, and both should be well greased before refitting.

Add Ferodo Premier brake pads to your calipers for maximum stopping power, but chamfer the pad edges to stop them squealing on the disc grooves. (Courtesy Paul Knight)

Remove the gear stick, and note the way the lockout plate fits beneath it. (Courtesy Richard Foks)

This is the accelerator cable. (Courtesy Richard Foks)

The handbrake cables must now be disconnected. They mount to the handbrake lever via cable adjusting nuts on all pre-1972 models, or to the equalizer bar thereafter. Here, the bar mounts to a pin on the bottom point of the handbrake lever, and is held by a spring clip that must not be lost when removed. On these models,

The clutch clevis pin is arrowed here at the centre, and can be difficult to remove. (Courtesy Richard Foks)

near the adjusters, the wire supports need to be disconnected to release the cables. These can then be left to hang downwards along with the clutch and accelerator cables.

Now engage either first or third gear, and turn to the gear linkage rod beneath the Bus. There's a gear coupling part way back along the length of the rod. Here the two parts are joined by a sleeve, which is bolted in place, and held by a lockwire. Cut the lockwire, then undo the bolt using penetrating oil, or even heat, to help loosen it if it won't move easily. With the gear lever removed from inside the cab, the gear rod can then be pulled towards the front of the van and released. The speedometer cable will also have to be released from the nearside front hub once the retaining cotter pin is withdrawn.

If you're taking the suspension

The handbrake cable pin. Do not lose the simple spring clip. (Courtesy Richard Foks)

assembly out, complete with hubs and track rods, only the draglink has to be disconnected from the swing lever that pivots on the centre pin located on the central bracket of the lower torsion tube. A ball joint splitter will be necessary to separate the tapered

Up by the handbrake adjusters, the wire supports must be disconnected before the cable can be released and left to hang down. (Courtesy Richard Foks)

pin of the ball joint connecting the draglink to the swing lever. You may also hit the end of the arm (not the thread itself) with a soft-faced mallet to 'shock' the joint into releasing from the locating eye. If you're intending to reuse the joint, don't damage the rubber seal or it will allow dirt to enter, and don't hammer on the end of the thread or it'll render the joint unusable.

Gear linkage rod must be removed, and can be pulled towards the front of the Bus once the lockwire and coupling are undone. (Courtesy Richard Foks)

It's always better to replace all such joints with new items and, when removing an old joint, note or mark the number of threads visible on the joint where it enters the sleeve. By fitting the new joint with the same number of threads wound back in, the steering geometry won't be lost when the suspension is reassembled. The joint also has a cotter pin running through a drilling in the end that prevents the castellated nut from moving. This should be removed (if it shears off, it may be necessary to drill it out) before the nut is wound off.

Only the draglink has to be disconnected from the swing lever if the suspension is to be removed complete with hubs and track rods. (Courtesy Richard Foks)

You may wish to remove the steering damper, to prevent any damage to it, when the beam is finally released, or simply replace it with a new item later. Any weight saving now will make the assembly easier to remove, as it's a very heavy item.

We have seen before how to remove the king and linkpin hubs. On the ball joint beam, the difference is that the steering knuckles are swivelled on upper and lower ball joints, with a smaller ball joint on the steering (pitman) arm. All of these joints will have to be released if the complete hubs are to be removed prior to the

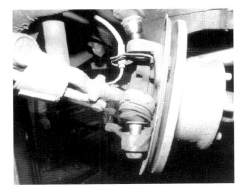

If the hubs are to be removed, the ball joints holding the stub axle and steering arm will need to be separated. (Courtesy Richard Foks)

Note the upper eccentric bush that sets camber at the front wheels. (Courtesy Richard Foks)

release of the torsion bar assembly. Whether they're drum or disc brake style is immaterial, as they're removed in very similar ways. Since we looked at drums on the rebuilt king and linkpin hubs we'll cover discs this time around.

With the hydraulic brake lines disconnected, the calipers can be released from the stub axles by undoing the two high tensile bolts from the rear and removing them. The calipers can be examined for wear, and the brake pads, retaining plates and spreader springs exchanged for new items. If there's any obvious damage to the rubber dust seals surrounding the pistons on either side of the caliper body, these will also need replacing.

Having removed the hub dust cap, an Allen key will release the bearing clamp nut and thrust washer ready to release the disc itself from the front wheel hub. This hub also carries the five-threaded road-wheel mounting lugs, and the disc is attached to it by two screws countersunk into the outer rim of the disc. Once removed, the disc and the hub can be withdrawn and the disc backplate also removed from the stub axle, which is now clearly visible.

Release the speedometer cable and place it out of the way. Use a 27mm combination spanner to undo

and remove the nut holding the upper torsion arm ball joint in place within the camber bush in the top stub axle eye. If the eccentric camber bushing turns (this is the bush used to adjust camber at the front wheels, and should always have the centre notch on the leading edge facing forwards when the wheels are in the straight ahead position. This gives the front wheels 0 deg 40´

With the dust cap removed, an Allen key can be used to release the bearing clamp nut. The thrust washer should have minimal play behind the nut upon reassembly. (Courtesy Simon Glen)

+/- 30´ of positive camber), use a 36mm open-ended spanner to hold it in place. With the top nut removed, slacken off the bottom ball joint nut, but leave it held to the ball joint pin by a few threads. Using a ball joint splitter - you may well need the long handled 'pickle fork' type for added leverage - release each ball joint from its tapered mounting. These are very tight, and may never have been removed, so be prepared for something of a struggle, but they'll eventually break the 'seal' between the matched surfaces. Once both upper and lower ball joints have been released, remove the bottom nut, and the whole assembly can be lifted away as a unit.

If you only wish to replace the torsion bar tube assembly with a new one (and these are available from suppliers like Heritage Parts in the UK, or Custom & Speed Parts in Germany, with or without height adjusters already fitted), and have not disconnected the flexible brake line, to keep the hydraulic system intact, hook the hub assemblies up with strong wire attached to the chassis to prevent the weight overstretching the brake hoses. You can also release the shock absorbers (these will probably require replacing by new items on reassembly, such as Spax, KYB or coil-over units in either stock or lowered form, depending on your other suspension modifications) to remove more weight.

Finally, remove the front stabiliser (anti-roll) bar by bending back the lock tabs on the metal locating brackets and knocking them off the clamps that secure the rubber bush and bar to the lower torsion arm. These clamps and the bushes should be replaced when reassembling, and you can choose either stock rubber bushes or high performance urethane items - particularly if you're fitting

**Replacement front axle beams are available, with or without height adjusters ready fitted.
(Courtesy Custom & Speed Parts)**

a heavy-duty front anti-roll bar to match a similar item at the rear. These performance bars are available from Just Kampers or Big Boys Toys in the UK, or Bus Boys in the US.

The four bolts that hold the axle beam to the front of the chassis on each side should be soaked in penetrating fluid, and gradually worked loose. Do not rush this part of the operation, as you don't want to shear one of these bolts off. It is unusual for the axle to simply drop out, but you must have a jack underneath the

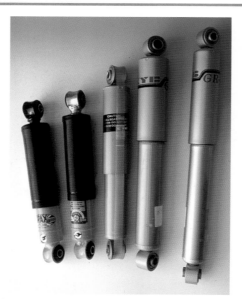

Performance shock absorbers such as Spax or KYB units in stock or lowered form can be chosen to enhance suspension upon reassembly.

bottom torsion bar to support it - just in case. The assembly will almost certainly require some persuasion to divorce itself from the chassis, but it will eventually come out.

**Heavy duty high performance front anti-roll bar and shock absorbers.
(Courtesy Just Kampers)**

With the suspension out, you can release the retaining lock nuts and dogtooth screws that locate each of the torsion arms to the torsion leaves within the top and bottom axle tubes.

The screws have an internal hex head and require a tool of exactly the same dimension to remove it, or you stand to strip the internal faces. It's also worthwhile cleaning these internal hex heads to remove any accumulated dirt prior to inserting the tool. This ensures a good, tight fit when applying leverage. Once released, the torsion arms can be moved to a workbench

Front anti-roll bar clamps and rubber bushes.

Four axle-retaining bolts are finally removed, after soaking in penetrating fluid.
(Courtesy Richard Foks)

Use a jack to support the beam as it is lowered from the Bus. (Courtesy Alex Leighton)

Ball joints must be pressed in and out of the torsion arms with an hydraulic press. Above is a '68-79 type. Below is an '80 - '91 type.
(Courtesy Custom & Speed Parts)

in order to replace the ball joints before we start work on the torsion beams in earnest.

REPLACING THE BALL JOINTS

Unless you have access to an hydraulic press, replacing the ball joints is one operation that you'll have to farm out to a garage or engineering shop. The ball joints should always be replaced if there's any sign of excessive ball joint play, or if the rubber seals have been damaged on removal, or dirt will enter the joint. Ball joint play is measured by pressing the stud in, all the way (in the arm), and taking a measurement with a vernier caliper. It's then pulled out as far as it will go, and a second measurement taken. Used ball joints must not exceed 2.00mm (0.080in), and new ones must not exceed 0.30mm (0.012in).

The joints must be pressed out on the hydraulic press, and new ones are press fitted into the torsion arms in the same way. If the eye of the arm has ever been oversized, due to wear, then oversized joints must be used. The torsion arms will be stamped with an embossed letter 'B' on them to indicate this, and the joints (0.30mm/ 0.012in oversized) have two additional V-shaped notches in them, but are otherwise fitted the same way, and are peened into the arm.

CHECKING THE SUSPENSION BEAM & HARRY HARPIC'S BEAM MODIFICATIONS

There are numerous ways you can modify the front beam for your performance Bus, and we'll look at the many options available. One of the most fundamental things is to work on a beam that hasn't suffered the ravages of rust or corrosion. Check the inside of the shock absorber towers for any signs of corrosion - you may be lucky, but some need minor repairs first. You may also wish to inject a rust inhibiting fluid such as Waxoyl into the uprights to prevent any further problems.

If the corrosion is bad, you have three options - either find a good replacement used beam; buy a new one (if you can find the correct type for

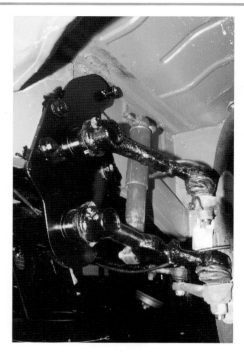

Harry Harpic's modified torsion beam with welded steel endplates to adapt late ball joint beams into earlier Buses.
(Courtesy Paul Knight)

your Bus); or consider a front beam modification from an engineering company, such as Harry Harpic's. Their experience with fitting 1968 - 1969 Bay-window ball joints and disc-braked front suspensions to earlier Buses and the increasing scarcity of parts caused them to seek an alternative option.

They discovered that post-'68 front suspension beams only differ from the earlier units, in that the outer needle bearings supporting the torsion arms are bigger in diameter. The inner metal bushings, however, are exactly the same diameter. The mounting points locating the beam to the chassis are also different. However, by completely removing the original (and often rotten) pressed steel front shock absorber towers, and welding on new specially machined and shaped thick steel endplates drilled to fit the earlier chassis mounts, the complete later beams could be made to fit into earlier chassis.

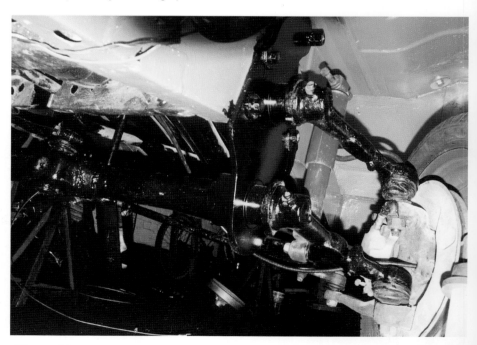

The modified beam can also be narrowed to prevent front inner wheel arch modification when lowering a Bus. (Courtesy Paul Knight)

An example of a 'tubbed' wheel arch to prevent tyre to body interference on a radically lowered Bus.

and have mounts drilled to suit the fixings in the earlier chassis, but also the torsion bar tubes themselves can have 30mm removed from each side to narrow the axles. By removing the original thick two-piece pressed steel shock absorber towers, the torsion tubes can be shortened and everything moved inboard without interfering with the original chassis rails.

This has been the problem on other wheel-to-arch modifications in the past. Of course, the torsion bars leaves also have to be shortened by the same amount, and must be re-drilled with the recesses at the outer ends to match the locating points of the torsion arm dogtooth grub screws. If you remove the leaves to perform this (or any other) modification, remember to make a note of which way round the leaves go, as they should always be reused in the same tubes and the same way round on refitting. This is simply because the torsional steel leaves take a 'set' with age, and could fracture if

Alternatively, by milling down the bearing surface of Bay-window Bus torsion bar arms by 6mm, they could be made to fit straight into earlier beams, and enhance Split-screen Buses with a ball-jointed front suspension and disc brakes. Since fitting a stock VW 1968-1969 front suspension to an earlier Bus has the undesirable characteristic of raising the front end, this modification does get round several problems at once.

It also allows one further modification. For the many Bus owners that want to lower their Buses radically, the front inner wheel arches have to be extensively modified (or 'tubbed') to prevent the tyres touching the bodywork. By modifying the later beam to fit into a Split-screen Bus, the shock absorber mounting plates can not only replace corroded metal,

Close-up of the inner skin of a Bus door to show the modification required to prevent wheel arch and tyre interference. (Courtesy Tobias Lindback)

Foksy adjuster is a non-ratchet design adjuster to raise or lower the Bus front suspension.

twisted the 'other way' around. The metal bearing seal retainers located at the outer ends of each tube must also be correctly re-installed over the new needle bearings, if you shorten the tubes. They must also have new rubber seals fitted to keep the bearings weather tight.

The flexibility of this conversion allows the original beam to be repaired and reused, rather than changing the whole assembly to effect a change. Late 5-stud drums or discs can be used on an early set up, and the availability of different disc styles also allows the use of 14in or 15in wheels. The 14in will automatically lower the Bus by approximately 1¹/₂in - 2in. You could even take the unlikely step of putting an early king and linkpin front suspension on to a Bay-window Bus with this option, though it would hardly be a performance modification!

FRONT BEAM ADJUSTMENT
Each set of torsion leaves is held by a dogtooth grub screw and locknut in the centre of each torsion bar tube. This makes it possible to lower (or raise) the front suspension by cutting a section from each tube (one at a time) and

rotating it by a set amount before re-welding it back together. By re-working a section in both upper and lower tubes by the same amount, the preload in the torsion bar leaves would not have changed. Only the relationship of the leaves within the tubes (and the torsion arms affixed to them at each end), would be different.

This was indeed the way that some of the earliest suspension modifications to Buses were carried out, but it has significant drawbacks. The movement of the leaves can't be adjusted again without completely re-working the beam every time a change is required. It also weakens the beam, and can create a harsh ride, as other suspension geometry is upset. However, it soon led to other ways of thinking about front suspension modification.

The Foksy front beam adjuster is one result of this type of new thinking. The adjuster developed by Bluebird Customs in the UK, works on the same principle as the Sway-A-Way adjuster on a Beetle. It still requires a section to be cut out of the top torsion bar tube and welded back in. As it only works on the one set of torsion bar leaves, it retains preload in the bottom leaves and gives a 'non-segmented' adjustment (i.e., non-ratchet design

Removing the stack of torsion leaves from the top torsion tube.
(Courtesy Alex Leighton)

adjuster) and a superior ride. It will lower the front of the Bus by up to 6in from stock height.

Since there is a lot of weight riding on the front suspension, fitting one of these adjusters is a skilled welding job, and must be done precisely and professionally to ensure that the

Clean up 6in either side of the grub screw hole all around the beam using a grinder, and mark the beam.
(Courtesy Alex Leighton)

modified beam is as strong as the original. If you prefer not to do this job yourself, find a competent engineering shop that can tackle this, or buy an exchange modified item direct from the manufacturers of this kit.

Fitting a Foksy front beam adjuster
The top beam (the one without the steering mechanism attached) is the only one that needs to be worked on with this type of adjuster. This is helpful in itself, as there's then no interference with the steering idler mounting on the lower torsion tube. With the stub axles and hubs already removed, undo the central lock nut and grub screw from the torsion tube so that the stack of torsion leaves can be slid out. They'll be covered in grease, so keep them together by wrapping them in a cloth,

**Cutting through the beam.
(Courtesy Alex Leighton)**

and make sure you know which way they'll go back in.

Now, using a grinder, clean up the centre of the torsion bar tube slightly more than 6in either side of the grub

**The centre section of the beam is cut through the centre stack at 90° to the screw, and is important for adjuster operation.
(Courtesy Richard Foks)**

screw hole, until you are back to bare metal all the way around the tube. Use a centre punch to mark the 6in distance either side of (and in line with) the centre screw hole. The reason for doing this is to establish the 'stock' position of the centre screw once the adjuster is fitted. Measuring from the centre of the grub screw, mark a position 20mm either side. You will now be cutting right through the tube at these marks, and the safest way

**Foksy adjuster welded to centre section.
(Courtesy Richard Foks)**

to do this is to use an industrial tube cutter (the type used by plumbers). If you only have access to hand tools, and will be using a hacksaw, firstly fit a jubilee clip (banjo clip) around the tube at the cutting position, so the edge acts as a guide for the hacksaw blade.

These cuts need to be absolutely straight, perpendicular and parallel, as the section of tube that's cut will have the adjuster welded to it, and will become part of the moving assembly. It may be necessary to move the jubilee clip to get the hacksaw blade past the tightening screw and keep the cut absolutely straight. Once the piece is released, carefully de-burr any roughness to the outer edges, and do the same on the torsion beam.

With the centre section of tube

cut out you'll see the shaped block within it, that the stack of torsion leaves passes through. In the Bluebird kit is a long bolt that now has to be wound into the original centre screw hole. With the centre section clamped in a padded vice, make a cut through the outer part of the tube and through the centre stack at 90 deg to the screw - this is important for the operation of the adjuster.

**Clamp the adjuster (welded to the centre section) and the rear plate in position on the beam, and tack weld them.
(Courtesy Alex Leighton)**

**Seam weld the parts all the way around the beam. The bump stops will also need removing on this conversion.
(Courtesy Richard Foks)**

The other parts of the kit include a semicircular-shaped plate that will be welded onto the back of the torsion tube, and another semicircular-shaped plate for the front. Onto these are welded two outer plates with crescent-shaped slots cut out of them. Into these semicircular-cutouts mount a cross bolt

An example of a Split-screen Bus at stock height (top), and lowered (above).
(Courtesy Jon Smith)

Just Kampers lowering adjusters are of the 'serrated type'.
(Courtesy Just Kampers)

attached to a plate, housing the long bolt and lock nut. The adjuster works when the lock nut and long bolt are loosened, the cross bolt slackened, and the cut centre section moved in one direction or the other to raise or lower the Bus.

With the centre section of the torsion tube mounted to the beam adjuster, clamp both this, and the rear plate, to the beam with the base of the adjusting slot in line with the punch marks you made earlier. 'One-man' clamps employing the 'mastic gun' ratchet system are ideal for this part of the operation. When you're happy that everything is in the correct position and fitting properly, tack weld the adjuster in place, making sure it operates freely.

Only when you're finally happy, seam weld it all around the beam to locate both front and back plates. You'll then have to wait for the beam to cool before you can refit all the torsion leaves back into the beam. These must go back in the same location as they were originally fitted, passing through the central mounting block. Make sure they are well greased before you do this as it will help keep the leaves together and make it easier for the stack to pass through the block. Once everything is together, don't forget to protect the new components

and welded joints with some anti-rust paint and a top coat for a properly finished appearance.

For this conversion, you'll need to cut off the beam's original bump stops, and fit some lowered shock absorbers. Other conversions retain the bump stops, so make sure you follow the manufacturer's instructions. The trailing arms can then be refitted, and the whole torsion bar assembly installed into the Bus. To help matters, brush some grease on the sides of the chassis members to help ease it into position as you raise it with a trolley jack. Line up the holes on either side (a screwdriver or tapered bar is very useful, as is a mallet to tap it into place) and finally replace the bolts.

If you need to replace any of the cables that run near the front suspension - such as the speedometer cable - now is the time! To reset the Foksy adjuster once the front suspension is fully re-installed and rebuilt, jack up the Bus under the centre of the front beam. Slacken off the cross bolt, then undo the central lock nut and long grub screw, to allow the centre part of the beam to move. Raise or lower the Bus (still on its wheels) until the desired height is reached, then tighten up the central grub screw, snug down the locknut and, finally, tighten the crossbolt, which holds the adjuster in the allotted place.

SERRATED LOWERING ADJUSTERS
The next type of front suspension adjusters we'll look at are the 'serrated' type. These allow adjustment to be made by moving the central torsion leaf retaining block up and down courtesy of a shaped metal plate with 'teeth' on its inner face. These interlock with a second plate welded to the torsion tube, with similar meshing

The weld around the mounting for the centre pin must be carefully ground away. (Courtesy Just Kampers)

Fitting Just Kampers' lowering adjusters

The first step, as before, is to remove the complete front suspension from the Bus, and to strip it down to the bare torsion tubes. For this conversion, though, both sets of torsion leaves have to be removed, as does the centre steering pin. Always check the beam completely for any signs of rot or corrosion before going any further, as any structural problems will have to be repaired, or a replacement beam found.

Offering up the adjuster, which must be carefully marked on the torsion tube. (Courtesy Just Kampers)

teeth on its outer face. By changing the relationship of one block to the other, the torsion leaves - and the arms - are moved and the ride-height of the front suspension is raised or lowered. With this conversion it is best practice to have the adjusters fitted into both the upper and lower torsion tubes to prevent any harshness to the ride.

The dimples indented into the torsion tubes mark the positions of the peens that hold the central leaf-retaining block, and must be carefully drilled out. (Courtesy Just Kampers)

The next job is to mark the location of the centre steering pin housing on the beam, as this will be removed when the adjusters are fitted. The pin is positioned in a metal bracket that's welded to the lower torsion tube. Use a centre punch, and make several marks to help you reposition it later on. There is a bead of weld that holds it on, and this will have to be very carefully ground away with an angle grinder. Don't use excessive force with the grinder, as you only want to break the weld, and you must not cut into the tube itself. If you prefer you can grind away most of the weld and then

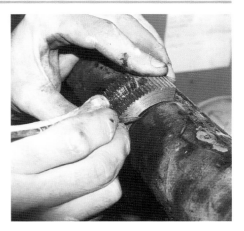

The positioning of the adjuster will determine the amount that the Bus can be raised or lowered. (Courtesy Just Kampers)

use a sharp cold chisel to break any remaining weld.

Once the housing is off, you'll see a small dimple indented into the torsion tube. This marks the position of a factory locking peen that holds the central leaf-retaining block within the torsion tube. In fact there are three such dimples around the circumference of each tube. You'll have to drill out each of these locking peens to release

The tube can be cut with a grinder, working inside the lines you have marked. (Courtesy Just Kampers)

the central mount so that it can rotate within the torsion tube. Either do this yourself, very carefully and accurately, on a pillar drill with variable speed, using a 10mm flat-bottomed drill or have an engineering shop do this for you. You want to drill out the material of the tube whilst causing as little damage to the central mount as possible. Use a cutting compound and as you work, continually back the drill off to prevent excessive heat build up, and allow the metal swarf to clear.

Now, working on one tube at a time, you need to locate the toothed adjuster. Use the threaded bolt through the adjuster to locate it to the central mount, then scribe a line around all four sides of the adjuster. Measure in 5mm from this line, and re-mark the shape onto the torsion tube. This marked area will be cut out, and it's therefore very important to cause no potential damage to the collar within the tube. The safest way to do this is to knock the collar to one side of the area that you'll be cutting. Since the locating peens have already been broken there's nothing to prevent it moving inside the tube. Use a suitably sized pipe that can be inserted into the end of the torsion tube, and bring it to bear on the central mount. It will be tight, but knock the collar to one side of the area you'll be cutting. Then, using a grinder fitted with a fine cutting disc, cut down the line at either side and across the top and bottom. Take it slow and steady, and don't cut beyond the lines you've marked.

When all four cuts have been made, remove the unwanted piece, and clean up the edges with a file, which will be easy to manoeuvre as the collar is situated to one side. Pick out any swarf or debris from the tube centre that will have stuck in the grease. Once the slot is de-burred, use the pipe to knock the central mount

back into its original position. Doing it this way (rather than with the collar still in situ) is also a good check on how easily the collar will move within the tube, as it must be free to rotate without sticking.

Place the toothed adjuster back on the beam and realign with the mount using the bolt. The adjuster provides about 50 deg of rotation, which equates to around 4in - 5in of travel at the wheel end. You can position the adjuster so that the beam can be totally lowered, raised or any other setting in between. Aligning the set screw hole in the centre of the adjuster will give you 2in - 2¹/₂in raised or lowered travel. If you want to go all the way down, position the adjuster

Finally welding on the adjuster. (Courtesy Just Kampers)

with more opening below the set screw hole - about 80% below and 20% above. To go this low, don't forget that you'll also need to modify or remove the bump stops (close to the base weld line), and use shorter shock absorbers.

Reverse this measurement if you want to go 4in - 4¹/₂in up.

Once you are happy with the positioning of the adjuster on the tube, tack weld it in place, then re-insert the bolt and double check that the central mount is still free to rotate. Finally check the alignment of the adjuster, and fully seam weld it onto the beam. Weld the adjuster by working in short ¹/₂in lengths to avoid possible heat build up and distortion, and keep checking that the central mount is free to rotate smoothly. You'll now have to repeat the process on the other tube, making sure that the two adjusters are fitted in the same position on each tube. Once both adjusters are welded in and the beam allowed to cool, the centre pin bracket can be offered up to the scribe marks made earlier on the lower torsion tube. It can then be tacked on once the beam is cleaned back to bare metal. When you're happy with the alignment, weld it on fully and, once cooled, apply some rust-inhibiting paint to the areas you've worked on.

The adjusters can now be assembled, using the Nylok and Allen bolt on the upper tube, for Bay-window Buses, or on the lower tube for Split-screen Buses. The whole suspension can then be reassembled ready for the unit to be refitted to the vehicle. If you've any problems refitting the stack of leaves through the central collar, divide the stack into two equal halves, and slide the bottom half into the collar. These go in very easily. Then, remove the very top leaf before sliding the other half in, and fit this last one on its own. You'll then need to rebuild the other parts of the suspension assembly, and bleed the brakes once the hydraulic lines are re-attached.

To set the ride height once the suspension is back in the Bus, simply

Kruizinwagon adjusters are available for either 1954 - 1967 or 1968 - 1979 Bus front suspensions. (Courtesy Simon Glen)

use a trolley jack beneath the centre of the bottom tube to take the weight off the road wheels. Then slacken the lock nuts before moving the toothed adjusters to the desired height and tightening them down. Never attempt to do this with the suspension under load. You'll also need to take the Bus to an alignment centre, or garage, to have the geometries of caster and camber checked before you use the Bus in earnest. Since the Bus will be running in a lowered stance for long periods, you'll need to check regularly

the condition of the ball joints, as these will tend to wear prematurely.

On very low Buses, you will have to ensure that tyre clearance is

Custom Bugs and Buses version of the adjustable bump stop mount – good news for Bus owners who don't want to lose this important original suspension feature. (Courtesy Simon Glen)

adequate, and it doesn't rub against the wheel arch or any suspension

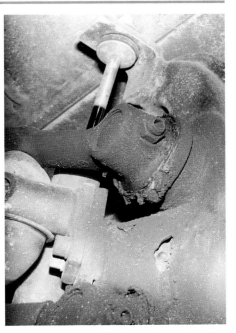

Kruizinwagon modified top shock absorber mount accepts shorter pin-style shock absorber. Lowered bump stop mount is also visible.
(Courtesy Simon Glen)

components. Low profile tyres can help achieve this, as can the choice of wheels. Later vans with the 5-bolt 112mm PCD disc or drum allow a greater ability to interchange wheels from other marques, and these will offer a variety of offsets to choose from. Find one that suits the look of your Bus and provides greater arch clearance.

A similar method of lowering Buses is offered by Australian VW specialist Indian Automotive, with the Kruizinwagon adjusters. These are available in two designs. One for 1954 - 1967 Split-screen Buses, and another for 1968 - 1979 Bay-window models. They have a similar ratchet principle to those above and are fitted in much the same way. The conversion does have a major advantage as it allows the retention of the original bump stops. This is achieved by welding a special plate in the position of the original

Kruizinwagon bumpstop adjusters fitted to a Bus torsion beam. The plate is movable and can be repositioned. (Courtesy Simon Glen)

Harry Harpic's front suspension adjusters use a movable central plate inside an outer metal bracket.

bump stop bracket, and mounting the latter to a new, and movable, bracket that bolts to the first plate. It can therefore be set at a standard ride-height position, or a lowered one, simply by unbolting it and moving it up or down.

This is good news as the bump stops are a very important part of the original beam and are quite often overlooked or disregarded and removed. As an added bonus, the company also modifies the top shock absorber mount to accept a shorter pin-style shock absorber, thereby increasing the available options. Fitting these adjusters is very much the same process as before, but always follow the manufacturer's detailed instructions.

Finally, in this section, is an adjuster that works on a slightly different design. Harry Harpic's design of Bus front adjusters use a shaped metal plate that welds to the centre of each torsion tube, and has a movable central plate inset into it. Each inset plate has two threaded holes (for the locking bolt) through it, but set at offsets to the overall length of the plate. The bolt can therefore be located into the central torsion leaf mount in one of two positions with the plate one way up, and another two with the plate turned upside down, giving a

total of four options. As with the other ratcheted adjusters, the central collar must be free to turn, but it is quite a novel slant on the otherwise very similar adjusters.

FITTING BUS BOYS' ALBATROSS ADJUSTERS

One of the best known types of front suspension adjuster available in the US is the 'Albatross adjuster'. It is available from Bus Boys and also distributed in Germany by Custom & Speed Parts. Whilst it essentially works on the ratcheted principle, as we've seen with other adjusters, the fitting is somewhat different. For that reason, I've covered this as a separate section to see exactly what is involved. Also, as with most of the adjusters covered in the book, these can be fitted in a way that will allow the Bus to be raised as well as lowered.

The kit allows the sets of torsion leaves to be adjusted in both the upper and lower torsion tubes. It consists of four ratcheted plates, the two top plates that engage into the ratchets, two centre holding screws and locknuts. There are also lockwires provided, that run through drillings in the centre screws preventing any possibility of the screws backing off, and allowing the top plates to move. As with the other fitting processes, this can only be done with the complete front suspension removed from the Bus, and with it stripped down to just the torsion bar tube arrangement, but with the torsion leaves still fitted.

Bus Boys Albatross adjuster kit. (Courtesy CSP)

Begin by removing both 19mm lock nuts that attach to the two 8mm hex factory centre screws locating the stack of torsion leaves within each torsion tube. Clean out the heads of the centre screws first, to prevent the hex heads being rounded by the hex tool you'll need to use, and then remove them. In their place, insert the new 4140 chromoly centre screws, using a $1/4$in hex tool, and tighten them down so that their dogtooth ends locate into the recess in the torsion leaf stack, inside the tube. The shaped metal top plate can now be slipped over the end of the screw, and will need to mesh its teeth with the two ratcheted plates that you'll place against the torsion tube.

Only work on one tube at a time for this part of the operation, and ensure that the teeth of the plates face the correct way to engage the top plate. The part number, embossed into the side of the ratcheted plates, should face towards the offside of an early RHD vehicle, and towards the nearside for a later RHD Bus. The ends of the ratcheted plates should be flush with the horizontal (bottom) edge of the top plate, before the lock nut is wound onto the centre screw, to snug the assembly down against the beam. Before the nut is fully tightened, press inwards on the ratcheted plates from both sides to press them hard up against the vertical surfaces of the top plate, until there is no lateral movement. The nut can then be tightened to hold all the parts in position.

Now, using the second top plate supplied in the kit, engage this into the ratchets that are still available behind the first plate. Get it as close as possible to the first top plate and double check that there is no lateral movement between either top plate and the ratcheted side plates. Using the centre

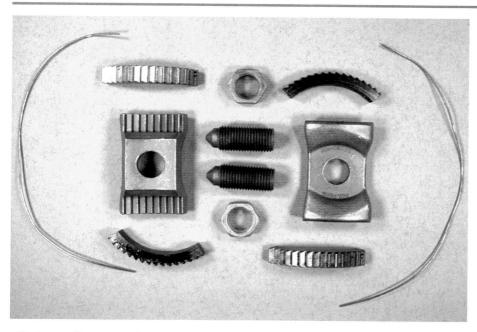

Albatross adjusters use lockwires to prevent any movement of the top plates in the teeth of the ratcheted plates.

possible to the idler bracket welds on the lower tube. Scribe lines onto the torsion tube along the outer edges of the ratcheted plates, and the exposed inner edges of the plates, making sure that the plates are pressed in hard against the vertical inner wall of the top plate. Remove the lock nut and top plate, placing the latter in the most raised position possible (i.e. as close to the idler bracket as is physically possible), then scribe a circle on the torsion tube through the centre screw hole. Using a ratcheted plate, complete the two scribe lines that join the centre screw to the scribed circle. The material within this area will be removed to make the slot for the centre screw.

The next part of the operation is to free the torsion leaf centre mounting blocks on each tube from their locating peens (marked by indents on the surface of the tubes), so the stacks of leaves can rotate. It is possible to carefully drill these peens out on a pillar drill, as we've seen with the fitting of previous adjusters, and to carefully knock the centre block to one side of the centre of the tube, whilst the drilling is done and the slots are being made on the tube. However, if you have access to the special 'rotating tools' available from Bus Boys in the US, you may wish to rent them from the manufacturer, and follow the next instructions on freeing the centre holding block from the factory peens.

Firstly, grind a slight taper to the four exposed ends of the stacks of torsion leaves. This is done partly to allow the fitting of the rotating tools - these are a pair of long tubes inserted from either end of the torsion tube and shaped to fit snugly over the stack of leaves, whilst accepting a 3/4in socket drive or breaker bar in the outer end to apply leverage - and also to allow easier insertion of the stack of leaves back through the central holding

hole in the second top plate, scribe a circle on the torsion beam beneath, then remove the lock nut and all the components from the beam except for the centre screw. The scribed circle will need to have a centre punch mark made at its very centre, which will act as a guide when drilling the material out. Also scribe two parallel lines on the tube between the scribed circle and the centre screw using one of the ratcheted plates as a guide.

This process must now be repeated on the other beam so that both are fully marked. All the material within these marks will be removed to give a 'slot' for the centre screw (holding the torsion leaves) to move within, achieving a lowering effect. This type of configuration will give a maximum of 54 deg of lowering adjustment, with each increment on the ratcheted plates giving a 6 deg change. A table of adjustments for this kit is given in the appendices.

For those wishing to raise - rather than lower - their Bus, the process up to this point is much the same, but obviously you want the ratcheted plates positioned lower than the original centre screw, rather than higher. The only issue is that whilst this doesn't present a problem with the upper torsion tube, the lower one has the steering idler bracket welded to it. This limits the location of the ratcheted plates to a position above it, giving a raising available on the lower torsion tube of between only 18 deg - 24 deg. This can only be enhanced by increasing the clearance of the idler bracket, which will allow further movement of the top plate and slot extension (though the ratcheted plates' positioning would remain the same). This isn't recommended as it weakens the idler mounting.

Assuming no modification to the bracket is to be made, the adjuster top plate must be located, as before, with the centre screw and lock nut, and with the ratcheted plates placed as close as block. You'll need two people for this operation, and plenty of muscle!

Place the torsion bar assembly on the ground, and insert a 5ft length of pipe, or wood, between the top and bottom torsion tubes. This will act as a brace to prevent the unit moving on the ground whilst pressure is put on the torsion leaf stacks to break the central peens. The brace must be capable of withstanding 1500ft/lb torque, so a metal brace is better. In this case, pad the ends of the brace or put wood between the brace and the torsion bar tubes, where it touches, to prevent denting them. A suitable brace would be 2in - 3in thick walled steel tubing, though you can use two braces, one at either end of the tubes, if you prefer.

The rotating tools must now be slid over the outer ends of the torsion leaf stacks at either end of the same tube. The tools must be slid home until they touch the sides of the centre holding block, which is 1in wide. Once on, the tools will leave the torsion leaf stacks 1/4in short of the inner edge of the fitting for the socket drive or breaker bar. If the tools don't slide fully home, remove them and check for any broken leaves or rust damage. This will have to be corrected before going any further. Any broken leaves must be replaced as a matter of course or the whole front suspension of the Bus could fail, and drop down on to the tyres. Incidentally you should **never** remove leaves from the front suspension to lower a Bus, as the total front weight will then ride on fewer leaves, and will ultimately fail.

Any rust between the individual leaves, causing the stack to widen and not fit into the rotating tool, will have to be cleaned off with the stack removed from the beam, and then re-inserted. Pay particular attention to the three large centre leaves on any stack whilst they are disassembled. These are the

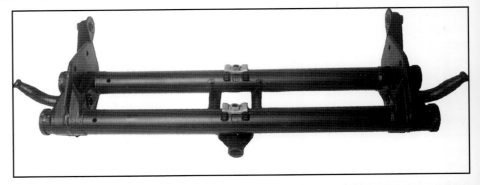

Fitted Albatross adjusters are of the 'serrated' type, and can be use to lower or raise the Bus front suspension. (Courtesy Custom & Speed Parts)

ones that have an indent in their outer edges to locate the dogtooth point of the centre screw, and ultimately locate the trailing arms. Any damage, or cracks, will necessitate them being changed before the stack is re-inserted into the beam. If the leaves don't need to be removed or replaced, remove both centre screws and lock nuts before rotating the centre block.

Once the socket drives or breaker bars are attached to the outer ends of the rotation tool, they can have a cheater bar (a 4ft - 5ft length of pipe to increase leverage) slipped over them. With one person rotating each tool, apply a progressive and equal pressure downwards to rotate the torsion leaf holding block free from its peens. This will take about 500ft/lb - 750ft/lb of pressure at each end. Don't rotate the block more than 45 deg, this will be enough to free it, otherwise, if it travels beyond 90 deg you risk damaging the thread of the centre screw hole as it passes the next set of peens. By rotating it first one way, then the other, the exposed peens can be hammered down to allow the block to move more freely. With the drive socket removed from the rotating tools, hammer against a wooden block held at one end of one rotating tool to knock the holding block to one side of the tube, so it clears the factory centre hole by 1/4in.

The rotating tool and stack of torsion leaves can now be removed and the operation carried out on the second torsion tube. When the whole operation has been conducted on both tubes, the beam assembly can be moved to a workbench for the drilling and cutting procedure. If you don't have a pillar drill, take the beam to an engineering shop and have them do this next part of the operation for you.

Begin by drilling a 1/4in guide hole through the centre of each circle you scribed and centre punched on the tubes. This can then be opened out to a 1/2in hole, and the slot can then be cut by relieving metal between the new hole and factory centre screw hole with an angle grinder. Try and get a slight chamfer on the edge of the slot, as this aids movement of the centre screw and top plate. Tap back the holding block to check for movement, and to ensure there are no internal burrs. By greasing the area as you cut, it'll catch swarf and minimise the amount of material falling back into the tube itself. Smooth any rough edges with a file, including the remaining thread at the far end of the factory screw hole. The slot should have a width of 0.555in - 0.557in, and the area around it should be cleaned back to bare metal ready to weld the ratcheted plates in place.

You may also wish to have the

whole beam professionally cleaned (chemically dipped) at this point, but if you do, ensure that the process won't damage the inner trailing arm bushings. Those on pre-1967 beams have phenolic and steel bushings and bearings normally unaffected by these processes, but those on the later beams are made of a soft metal called babbit, and could be damaged.

Prior to welding, you'll have to knock the centre block back to its central location. This can be done by installing the greased stacks of torsion leaves, refitting the rotating tool, and tapping it on the outer end with a hammer and woodblock, until you locate the centre screw recess back to its original position. With the holding block in its original factory location, offer up the ratcheted plates, and top plate as before. Then insert the new centre screw, in the Albatross kit, so it locates the torsion leaves, and fit the lock nut, torquing it down to 29ft/lb.

Do the same on the other tube ensuring that the ratcheted plates fit comfortably against the vertical inner edges of the top plates. The plates are now ready to be welded and you may wish to have this done professionally, since the strength and integrity of the whole beam now rests on the quality of this part of the operation.

Move the centre screw 0.025in up from the bottom of the slot. This small measurement allows the centre screw to be moved backwards by this amount, releasing the top plate after welding. If you're happy there's no lateral movement of the ratcheted side plates, tack weld on the outer surface at each end of the plates, repeating the process on the other beam.

Remove the lock nuts and top plates, then run a fine bead of weld on the inner edges of the ratcheted plates, not allowing it to rise above half the height of the plate itself or it will

interfere with the bevels on the flanges of the top plate. On the outer edge there's no such restriction, and the height of the weld can extend almost up to the meshing teeth of the plate. Each end of the plates can be welded to the beam for additional strength. Once both adjusters are welded into position, check the movement of the top plates through all positions and that the top plate engages the teeth of the ratcheted plates, without any problems. Minor grinding of the bevel of the top plate can be accommodated to ensure a final fit if necessary.

The final job is to drill a small $1/16$in hole in the lower outside corner of the right ratcheted plate to allow the safety wire to pass through. The other end runs through the hole in the centre bolt, as a fail-safe device to prevent any movement of the adjuster once it is located in position.

Finally, the whole beam can be reassembled, painted and refitted to the Bus. To make adjustments to the suspension settings with the Albatross adjusters fitted, raise the front of the Bus and place it firmly on axle stands. This relieves all torsional pressure on the top plates so that they can be released by loosening the lock nuts, once the safety wires are removed from the centre screws. Since the top plate is designed to mesh into the serrated teeth of the outer plates, it can be released by simply pushing down on one of the trailing arms.

With the Bus lowered to the required height (or the trailing arms raised to give the same effect), the top plate can be engaged in the desired position. The same adjustments should be made to both upper and lower adjusters to prevent preloading one set of torsion leaves. Once the position is decided, the top plates should be engaged into the teeth of the outer plates, the lock nut torqued down to

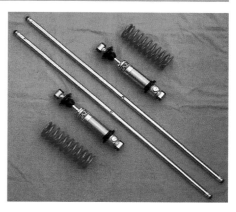

Red 9 Design EZ Rider front end lowering kit. (Courtesy Red 9 Design)

29ft/lb, and the safety wires refitted.

If the Bus has been substantially lowered, don't forget to fit shorter shock absorbers. You may also need to reposition the mountings for the rubber bump stops. It's not advisable to drive your Bus without them, and they're there for a reason! Depending on the final ride height at which you set your Bus, the manufacturers of this conversion also retail what are known as 'Spring Stiffeners' to help prevent excessive movement of the trailing arms and wheels. These help stiffen the torsion leaves, and are especially important for radically lowered Buses, as the wheels may otherwise interfere with the wheel arch of the body. On any Buses that have their front suspension modified it's advisable to regularly inspect the torsion leaves to check for any that have cracked. Finally, as with any such modification, always have your suspension geometries checked at a garage to get the best out of your newly modified suspension.

RED 9 DESIGN EZ RIDER FRONT END LOWERING KIT
If you prefer not to cut and weld the front torsion bar tubes to install height adjusters, then the Red 9 Design

'EZ Rider' front end lowering kit is a noteworthy alternative. There are no specialist tools required to fit this kit, which consists of two tie bars that run within the torsion tubes and replace the original torsion-leaved bars.

Lowering is achieved by utilising adjustable dampers with coil-over springs. The coil-over springs are set to give the appropriate drop required (100mm or 60mm), and this must be specified when ordering these parts. The springs are rated to maintain the ride quality at the front of the Bus, and special spring rates can also be requested for non-standard applications. The dampers allow fine tuning of the ride, whilst the reduced ride height gives improved handling to the Bus, and there's no loss of steering lock with standard wheels. The tie bars come pre-assembled and, once fitted, are enclosed within the torsion tubes for a cleaner look, with the option to return the parts to original, if required later. Since no cutting or welding of the beam is required, these parts are also easy to fit, and the front suspension doesn't need to be completely removed from the Bus.

Fitting the EZ Rider lowering kit

Begin the operation by jacking up the Bus and setting it on axle stands, then remove the road wheels. Working on one side only, disconnect the flexible brake hose, and clamp it to avoid loss of brake fluid. You'll also need to remove the ball-jointed track rod end from the steering (pitman) arm on the stub axle and, if you're working on the front left side, the speedometer cable as well.

Both shock absorbers can now be completely removed, to be replaced with the new items upon reassembly. Slacken the lock nuts and dogtooth grub screws that hold the stacks of

torsion leaves within the torsion tubes. There are six of these - one in the centre of each torsion tube, and one holding each of the four trailing arms.

You'll now be able to draw the hub assembly, complete with the trailing arms, from the side you've been working on. Once removed, the ends of the two stacks of torsion bars are visible, and can be withdrawn. Since these are covered in grease, they should be wrapped up and marked, in case they are ever needed again to return the Bus to stock. All torsion leaves should only be fitted in the tubes one way, as they take a 'set' with

Baja Buses are common in Australia and give great off-road potential. (Courtesy Simon Glen)

age, so marking them is important.

With the grub screws removed, the new EZ Rider trailing arm tie bars can be slid into the torsion tubes, taking care that the centre dimples in the bars are aligned with the grub screws in the centre of the beam housing. Tighten the grub screws firmly, and secure them with the lock nuts, as originally fitted.

The whole trailing arm and hub

assembly that was removed can now be refitted, ensuring that it's aligned correctly on the new tie bars so that it slides into place. You may need to tap it with a soft-faced hammer to locate the trailing arms exactly over the dimples in the tie bar, and then the four grub screws can be refitted into each of the trailing arms. It's important that these grub screws are tightened down firmly, as the point of the grub screw must locate into the 'v' groove of the bronze bushes mounted at the ends of the trailing arm tie bars. Once seated correctly, the grub screws should be slackened off 1/4 turn and the

lock nuts tightened down. This allows the trailing arms to be free to pivot and be properly located.

The coil-over springs and dampers can now be mounted in place of the original dampers that you removed earlier. For Buses with king and linkpin front suspensions, you'll also need to install the extra 'lower coil-over mount' provided in the kit. These are 'handed', and should be mounted

Split-screen and Bay-window Buses look good 'raised up', and generally retain better suspension geometry than lowered equivalents. (Courtesy Simon Glen)

front dipping downwards, as it would upon heavy braking. The nose down stance of a Bus lowered more at the front than back can therefore upset the valve, as it thinks the Bus is continually braking, and is therefore trying to apply more pressure to the back brakes. If you notice this tendency, you'll have to compensate by adjusting the bracket (inside the left-hand chassis rail) that locates the valve. This can only be done with the Bus being tested on a brake roller to find the optimum performance of the valve.

RAISING THE FRONT SUSPENSION

It may seem from the conversions that we've already looked at that there's only one way to go with a Bus suspension, and that's downwards - but it's not so. There are plenty of Bus owners and drivers who want to do just the reverse, and raise the suspension. Obviously, the adjusters

with the rear end turned as high up as possible.

With the components fitted, you'll now need to refit the track rod ball joint to the steering arm (or replace it with a new one if the rubber seal has been damaged), reconnect the speedometer cable and re-plumb the brakes before bleeding them, to purge any air in the system. The road wheels can be refitted, and the Bus should then be taken to a tyre shop to have the whole front-end suspension geometry checked and adjusted. The dampers can, of course, be adjusted to fine tune the ride on the Bus, but that's it! It really is an easy and economic answer to the problem of getting a Bus 'down' in the front, and making it handle.

One last point concerning late, lowered, Buses that came with factory fitted disc brakes is that they have a brake bias valve within the braking system that can cause problems. This is purely on Buses that have been severely lowered at the front, and thus 'tip forward', and not those at stock

height, or lowered (but level) Buses. The bias valve basically helps the braking system apply more pressure to the rear brakes when it senses the

A thick steel plate is normally welded to the axle beam flange to 'lift' the body about 4in from the suspension. (Courtesy Simon Glen)

we've already seen will raise Buses as well as lower them, but for more serious off-road use, there's another way. Keep the components of the front suspension absolutely stock (and why not ? - VW designed them to be incredibly strong), but simply change the relationship of the suspension to the chassis.

The most common way of converting to a 'Baja Bus' is to fabricate new thick steel plate mounts and weld them onto the torsion beam housing (one at each end), behind the shock absorber mounts - near the original beam to chassis mounting holes. These plates are shaped to extend approximately 4in upwards from the suspension and meet the original mounts on the chassis, raising the front of the Bus by this amount. Whilst it's possible to raise this still further by using an adjustable beam, this is probably enough for most people. The only consideration here is to ensure your flexible brake lines are long enough to accommodate the changes in height, when the suspension is working at its furthest extent.

Different variations to raise the front suspension can be seen on Buses

The increase in body height does not increase ground clearance, but improves front and rear approach on rough terrain. (Courtesy Simon Glen)

in the Australian outback, and depend on the ingenuity of the builder. Some may be a more boxlike mounting than simply two steel plates, but the principle is still the same. This method doesn't increase ground clearance (which is good on a Bus anyway) but it does improve front and rear approach and departure angles when negotiating rough terrain. Making this modification shouldn't upset steering geometry, and is a reversible modification in most cases - unlike raising a front suspension by cutting, turning and re-welding the centre part of the two torsion tubes. This latter modification is not only a permanent change, but can cause problems with the front suspension geometry, as it allows insufficient movement for the track rods.

WHEELS AND TYRES

With more tyre to wheel arch clearance, it's the perfect opportunity to think about fitting larger wheels such as 15in Mercedes rims, and off-road tyres, increasing the back county potential. Even alloy wheels such as the Mercedes 17in with 5-bolt fittings in a 5 x 112mm PCD style can also be bolted straight on to the 1971 - 1979 Bay-window Bus without problems.

Aftermarket wheels such as the Wolfrace Racelight design not only

Fitting larger wheels (in this case 15in Mercedes rims) has meant cutting away small parts of the front and back of the wheel arch. (Courtesy Simon Glen)

come in a 17in size, but can be drilled in a 5 x 112mm PCD (the same as the Mercedes), and with a 37mm offset, this places them perfectly within the wheel arch of a Bay-window Bus. The only consideration being the use of longer wheel studs (available from companies such as Machine 7), and a 4mm spacer - purely to allow the centre caps of the wheels to clear the speedometer cable fitting on the hub. For road use, when fitted with a 205/40 x 17 tyre, the rolling radius is similar to the original, and will therefore require no re-calibration of the speedometer. For off-road use, taller tyres will affect your speedometer, and

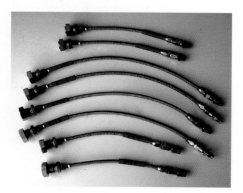

When raising the Bus, use longer flexible brake lines to accommodate the change in suspension height. Braided stainless steel brake hoses not only look good, but are of a superior quality for better performance.

Cut and turned front suspension raises the front of this Bus.

Wolfrace Racelite 17in rims in a 112mm PCD and 37mm offset place them perfectly within this bay-window Bus wheelarch. (Courtesy Paul Knight)

Hi-rise Buses have a style all their own! Just add some graphics for the final custom touch. (Courtesy Simon Glen)

your gearing, so be prepared for other adjustments.

Though the smaller wheel bolt pattern on the later Buses is an advantage, wheel adaptors have now become available for all models, allowing the interchange of a large number of stock, custom, and after market alloy wheels from other manufacturers. This increases the opportunities to customise your Bus even further, and without necessarily breaking the bank if you shop wisely for second-hand wheels. They may even complement other changes to the Bus, and everything from Mercedes front brake discs to Alfa Romeo brake calipers have been seen tucked within the wheel arches of modified Buses. We'll look at some of the wheel and tyre options in the next chapter. Where the VW Bus is concerned there seems to be no end to the levels of ingenuity and engineering available for these vehicles.

Wheel adapters allow a wider range of custom and aftermarket wheels to be fitted to your Bus – just add your imagination.

Chapter 3

Rear suspension & brakes

In this chapter we will be looking at the Transporter's rear suspension and braking system, and what opportunities are available to improve the basic design. There have been two designs of suspension used since the Bus was first introduced, the swing axle suspension, and the IRS (Independent Rear Suspension). The former appeared in Split-screen Bus designs (T1) from inception through to the 1967 model, whilst the IRS appeared on the T2 Bay-window models between 1968 -1979, and the T3 'wedge' range (also popularly known as the Type 25) from 1979 onwards. Whilst the IRS suspension provides undeniably better roadholding, and was introduced by VW to comply with

Reduction gearboxes at the outer ends of the axles take loading off the gears in the main case and provide extra ground clearance.

Exploded view of the reduction gearbox internals

greater safety regulations in its main markets, the earlier design can also be improved. Let's start with this swing axle design.

SWING AXLE SUSPENSION

VW's first production models of the Transporter used the swing axle design for good reason. It was readily available from their Beetle saloon. It was strong and durable, economical to manufacture ,and with some modification, it could be pressed into service straight away.

By adding reduction gearboxes to the outer ends of the axles, in a style similar to the military Kubelwagen, the loading was taken off the gears in the main case, making the unit suitable to accommodate the strains placed on it by a commercial vehicle. Since the reduction boxes reversed the gearing, the ring gear within the main gearbox

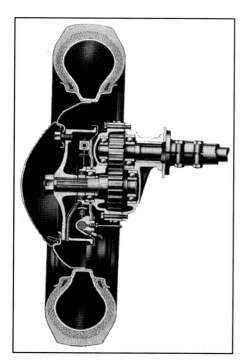

Cutaway of the rear transporter brake drum and reduction box, showing the axle shaft, driven shaft and gears.

case was swapped to the other side to give a standard four forward and one reverse gear.

The layout also provided an extra 3in ground clearance and gave the option of altering the gearing of the Transporter, by changing gears in the reduction boxes without complete disassembly of the main gearbox. A ratio of 1.39:1 (number of teeth: 25/18) was used for the 1200cc model though other variants were used by VW in Europe, including a 1.68:1 for mountain use. From August 1963, a ratio of 1.26:1 (number of teeth: 24/19) was used for the 1500cc and 1-ton models. Later units (from chassis 1 144 303) are identifiable by the 46mm rear hub nut (the early ones were 36mm), and the seal at the rear of the reduction box housing, which allows easier removal of the reduction gear shaft and bearing.

Drivers of swing axle Buses will notice that the rear suspension gets stiffer and the rear of the vehicle rises upon acceleration. This movement is simply because of the torque reaction of the main axle shafts turning one way, and those of the reduction boxes the other. With the wheel centre lower than the spring plate pivot on the torsion bar, and the upright design of the reduction boxes, any rotation of the short reduction gear axle shafts tries to rotate the plates downward and forward, thus raising the rear of the vehicle. The rear remains held up by the oscillating spring plates whilst power continues to be applied, and effectively stiffens the rear suspension. This is a useful feature for a loaded commercial vehicle pulling away from stationary, but not always appreciated on daily driven Buses.

REDUCTION BOX OIL CHANGE

It is a strong design but bearings within

the reduction boxes should be checked periodically and the gear oil, within the gear housing, should be changed every 30,000 miles (it has a wholly separate oil supply to the main gearbox). For a simple gear oil change (the reduction gearbox casings have a drain plug at the bottom and a filler at the top of the cast iron casing), undo the plug with a hex-headed key and simply drain the old oil and replenish with SAE 90 Hypoid gear oil (0.53 US pint, 0.44 Imperial pint, 0.25 litres).

Reduction box overhaul

Separating the two parts of the bolted together reduction boxes and inspecting the bearings and gears is a bigger operation. The first job is to undo the 36mm rear axle nuts (46mm on post '63 models) that locate the rear brake drums. Since these are torqued to 217ft/lb (30mkg), or 253ft/lb (35mkg) on the later models, the Bus should be on its wheels for this part of the operation. Withdraw the split pin that passes through the castellated hub nut (a new one will be used on reassembly), and turn the nut with a suitably sized socket on a drive, with extra leverage provided by a long extension bar or scaffolding pipe slipped over it. An alternative is to use a tool such as the Torque-Meister (see tools section). Once the nuts are loosened on both sides, the rear of the Bus will have to be raised with a trolley jack, ideally with a capacity of 2 tons or greater, and set on sturdy axle stands.

The road wheels can now be removed, followed by the axle nuts and then the brake drums, which spline to the outer ends of the driveshafts. Release the handbrake, and back-off the leading and trailing brake shoes by inserting an adjuster (or screwdriver) through the small hole in the front of the brake drum and turning the adjusters positioned at the top of the assembly. The drum will then slide off the shaft. The brake shoe locating springs and cups can be pressed down and turned to release them from their retaining pins, and the return springs unclipped using pliers. The return springs on some Transporters are in pairs hooked into holes in the backplates. The eye of the handbrake cable will have to be unhooked from the brake lever arm, and the lower handbrake locating rod freed, before the two shoes can be pulled from their mountings in the star adjusters at the top, and the wheel cylinder at the bottom.

All parts should be inspected for wear and replaced before reassembly, if required. To release the handbrake lever arm from the shoe, a horseshoe clip will have to be pried off, and replaced when re-attaching to a new brake shoe. Models prior to March 1955 (1200cc) had brake shoes of 40mm width (1.58in) in drums of 230mm (9.06in) diameter. The lining thickness on new shoes is between 0.188in to 0.196in. After this date, rear wheel cylinders were enlarged from 19.05mm (0.75in) to 22.2mm (0.87in) to match the increase in diameter of the master cylinder. However, this remained as a single circuit brake system, albeit with front and rear circuits made independent from 1963, by utilising a tandem design. Later 1500cc models had 45mm (1.78in) shoes within 247mm (9.85in) diameter drums.

Since the pressurised brake system remains intact, and hasn't been opened at any point, either put a brake pipe clamp on the flexible brake hose behind the backplate, or put a wire loop around the pistons of the wheel cylinder. This will prevent them from being ejected if the foot brake pedal is pressed. The brake backplate is held in place by a central bearing cover, which

New bearings, gaskets and rear plugs are available for reduction boxes from specialist suppliers.

must be released by unbolting four retaining bolts. A paper gasket behind it will be replaced on reassembly. An oil deflector and oil seal will remain in the cover as it's withdrawn, but both will require replacement.

Early models, which use this deflector, also have an oil drainage tube fitted inside the brake drum. Later versions use an oil flinger (like a large washer) that forces any leaking oil back to the bearing and away from the drum internals. The bearing cover has a lug and drilling at the bottom, matched by the paper gasket, that allows any oil seepage to drain away behind the backplate. The backplate can be pulled over the end of the shaft and held by a support wire so that the brake line doesn't over stretch. The handbrake lever can also be detached, if necessary, to give more play by removing the anchor pin circlip at the front of the Transporter.

The metal outer spacer can be pulled from the axle shaft, followed by the small rubber sealing ring and washer (1200cc models only). You will then need a bearing puller to draw the bearing from the shaft, followed by another spacer. The reduction gearbox housing can now be opened to examine the gears for wear, and to replace the inner bearings.

All the bolts holding the two case halves together must be removed, and the outer casing cover tapped with a soft hammer to part it from the inner casing. This is located by the driveshaft (axle) tube and is also bolted to the spring plate, as well as forming the mounting to which the shock absorber is attached at the bottom. A paper gasket between the two halves will need to be replaced when the unit is rebuilt (use a gasket sealant too), and these are available from specialists such as Wolfgang International or BBT.

Early (left) and late (right) reduction box design. The later models (1963-1967) use an end cap plug at the rear of the casting to access the driven shaft bearing.

1144303 (rear axle no. 6002091) were fitted with driven gear shafts of 35mm diameter to provide added reinforcement, which replaced the earlier 30mm diameter design.

If bearings are to be replaced, the new items must be driven into the casing squarely with a drift before the rest of the components are reassembled in a reverse of the disassembly procedure. Fit the drive gear and its outer bearing, renewing the circlip if it has weakened. Once the two halves of the housing are fitted together with a new gasket between them, the bolts can be evenly torqued down and finally new oil added to the rebuilt cases.

The brake assemblies will also need to be rebuilt using new shoes and internal parts such as the return springs to optimise performance. If

Work on the axle shaft first (the top one) and use strong circlip pliers to spring off the bearing retaining circlip. Now the bearing can be drawn off the shaft with a puller, and the reduction drive gear removed. This top outer bearing is a smaller size than the upper and lower inner bearings, so make sure you get the correct replacement parts. The inner bearing should be examined for wear in situ and if there's any sign of play it will also have to be drawn off the shaft with a puller. Finding one with long enough arms and fine 'claws' that will lock into the bearing rim is difficult though.

Moving to the reduction gear shaft, pull this out from the bearing into which it is press fitted. Later models use a circlip to locate the bearing, and a locking nut that secures the inner bearing race to the shaft. This has to be removed by accessing it through the end cap plug at the rear of the housing, This is only visible once the spring plate is unbolted from the reduction

box casing. A tip here is to tack weld a nut to the original plug and screw a slide hammer into it, using the tool to work the plug out. Grind off the tack weld, and the plug is reusable. However, if it's damaged, new ones are available from Alan Schofield in the UK or Wolfgang International in the US. Check the bearing in situ first, as an unworn item doesn't need replacing. Now check the reduction drive gears for wear and damage. The shafts of the later models require pressing out of the casing using an extractor worked from the back of the casing.

Excessive wear of the gears, or any cracking, will render the reduction box noisy and ineffective. In these cases, replacement will be the only answer, though finding NOS (New Old Stock) or quality replacement parts is becoming very difficult. Also ensure that any replacement shaft matches the original in terms of the gearing, and the diameter. Transporters from chassis

New brake shoes and wheel cylinders should be used when rebuilding your brakes to optimise performance.

there's any sign of brake fluid leaking from the wheel cylinder, then that will also need replacing. Once the brake system is 'opened' (to replace any part) then the whole brake system will need to be bled to remove any air that will have got into it. The brake system will otherwise be ineffective at best, or possibly downright dangerous as the trapped air will compress and the brake fluid will not apply the brake shoes to the drum surfaces.

STRAIGHT SWING AXLE CONVERSION

The reduction boxes may be adequate for many Bus drivers, but those who are looking for gearing that is more suited to driving on today's highways, higher mpg, or who simply want fewer parts to wear out, can consider other alternatives. There are many companies now offering 'off-the-shelf' solutions to the needs of Bus owners who want to change their rear suspension setups, or who simply wish to lower the rear of the Bus for aesthetic purposes.

The only disadvantage of removing the original reduction box setup is that since you'll no longer have the gears within the boxes slowing the Bus, this will therefore cause engine revs to be lower. The engine braking effect on deceleration will therefore be less, and there will be greater brake pedal pressure required to apply the same braking to the drums. Make sure you do this conversion as part of a more detailed brake and suspension overhaul, and you'll not notice it too much though. Since the back will be lowered, you'll also need to modify

the front suspension to match, making it a major overhaul of the complete suspension on your Bus.

With any modifications to the Bus suspension, remember that you're altering what is a very efficient system, and one that's been designed by VW to work within certain design constraints. For example, the rear suspension is designed to work within certain travel limits, so if you plan on lowering it extensively, to 'slam' the Bus to the floor, you'll be radically altering the geometry, and such extremes need to be carefully planned.

The more you lower a Bus (particularly a Split-screen Bus) the more it toes in and, whilst a certain amount of toe in is part of the original factory setting, measurements of toe in/out and rear track are critical to maintain a vehicle that handles well. The VW Bus rear geometry may be unusual even in stock form (compared to other vehicle engineering principles), but it does work well. Stay with as many original VW derived parts and suspension geometries as possible and stick to the old adage 'if in doubt, make it stout'. There's a lot riding on that suspension!

We'll start with a Beetle 'straight swing axle conversion', available in the US from Wolfgang International or Bus Boys Inc, or in Europe from Custom & Speed Parts. This kit provides all new mounting hardware for installation, and special parts including the spring plates, ready to accept the Beetle long axle tubes in place of the Bus reduction box items. Alternatively, a kit allowing the original Bus spring plates to mount to the swing axle Beetle axle tubes with shaped adaptor plates is also available from UK firm, Harry Harpic's, and uses as many VW parts as possible to keep prices lower.

These conversion kits replace the axle/reduction box assemblies with

Harry Harpic's shaped adaptor plates allow the original Bus spring plates to mount to Beetle axle tubes.

new, long axle tubes from a 1968 or later swing axle Beetle, or a pre-1965 swing axle VW Type 3 (Fastback/Squareback/Notchback). These have the 'longer' axles, together with the longer outer splines, and complete brake assemblies that are necessary for this conversion. By removing the reduction boxes, the rear of the Bus will automatically be dropped approximately $3\frac{1}{2}$in. You can either retain your original Bus gearbox and fit the new axles to it - in which case the ring gear inside the gearbox case will need to be moved from one side to the other - or simply replace the

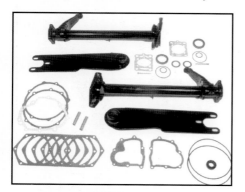

Custom & Speed Parts straight axle conversion kit.
(Courtesy Custom & Speed Parts)

Lowering a Bus extensively looks cool, but can create wheel removal problems.
(Courtesy Tobias Lindback)

complete transaxle with the swing axle Beetle/early Type 3 unit. In either case it'll be necessary to remove the original transaxle.

Before you start, bear in mind that, whilst the conversion allows you to drop the Bus lower than an IRS conversion, it will also create subsequent problems with rear wheel removal, and can also drain gearbox oil from the outer hub bearings if they are inclined into excessive negative camber.

Fitting the straight swing axle conversion

With a job like this it always makes sense to soak the nuts, attaching the spring plates to the back of the reduction boxes and the nuts and bolts mounted to the shock absorber, with a penetrating fluid, as they are usually seized solid. Use WD-40 or an oil/paraffin mixture, and leave them to soak overnight. Tightening a clamp around the end of the spring plate will also make it easier for the bolts to be withdrawn from the reduction box casing. The clamp will hold the plates

Gearshift rod couplings. (left) is early Bus item; (right) is for later models and is available as a stronger, urethane item.

up and prevent their preload pulling downwards and stripping the threads of the bolts.

While the oil is working, there are other items that can be undone. As a safety precaution, the battery earthing strap must be undone for any operation that involves removing the engine. The engine removal process is not detailed here, and a workshop manual should be consulted for this procedure. The electrical cables from the starter motor can be removed - the starter remains attached to the gearbox - when the assembly is out of the vehicle. The handbrake cables must also be released from their mountings at the handbrake lever by undoing the lock and adjusting nuts. The underside of the handbrake lever and the cables can be accessed beneath the vehicle by removing the cover plate under the pedal cluster. The cables can then be pulled free from their mountings ready to be drawn back through the guide tubes when the transaxle is removed. The clutch cable can also be disconnected from the operating lever on the gearbox, and

the rubber boot and flexible guide tube disengaged from the boss on the left-hand final drive cover. The gearshift rod coupling can be undone beneath the Bus by releasing the locking safety wire through one of the screws and unscrewing it. The gear lever in the cab can be moved forward to disengage the coupling from the gear selector rod. This coupling should be renewed upon reassembly, as a worn part

Choose wheels for a lowered Bus carefully – these Porsche wheels on a limo Bus clear the arches, and look just right!

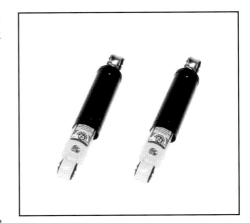

**Spax replacement adjustable dampers are available from Custom & Speed Parts, and Red 9 Design.
(Courtesy Custom & Speed Parts)**

can give imprecise gear changing. It is a different design from the Beetle (Type 1) coupling on the early Buses, so it will have to be sourced from a specialist supplier.

The penetrating/dismantling oil should have worked by now, so undo the shock absorber mounting bolts top and bottom. The shock absorbers (dampers) will be exchanged for new ones, with less travel, to account for the lowering process at the rear. Adjustable dampers made specifically for this purpose are available from Red 9 Design in the UK. They are a direct replacement for the stock item and give a 30-position adjustment, via a control knob, as well as having an integral bump stop.

With the clamp over the axle tube and under the spring plates holding it up, bend down the locking tabs on the bolt heads, and undo the four spring plate mounting bolts. Repeat the process on both sides. Finally, make sure that the accelerator cable is unhooked from its retainer on the gear carrier. You're then free to place a trolley jack beneath the transaxle to take its weight as the mounts at the end of the frame fork, and front of the transmission housing, are undone. The whole unit can be carefully pulled towards the rear of the Bus, and then lowered to the ground.

In this conversion, since both the axle tubes and the spring plates (which have elongated holes drilled in them to allow toe-in/toe-out setting) will be changed or adapted there is, unfortunately, little point in making chisel marks on both items for later reassembly, as you would otherwise do. Toe-in will therefore have to be reset with accurate measuring equipment at a garage. However, it's worth using a protractor to take an accurate measurement of the angle of the spring plate whilst it's still at rest

Bus gearbox nose cone will need to be fitted to the Beetle unit.

on the metal rebound stop and before it's unloaded of tension. Assuming the chassis is level, the plate can be measured again after releasing it off the stop, and these measurements used to set the angle of the new spring plate. Also take a measurement from the outer end of the axle tube forwards to a point on the chassis and make a note of this, as it'll help you reset the rear toe in/out alignment. You will still need a check by a local tyre shop, when everything is back together, to ensure 100% accuracy.

The new kit comes complete with replacement spring plates, axle tubes, and the necessary seals and gaskets. Assuming you're exchanging the original unit for the replacement Beetle, or early Type 3 unit, the first job will be to take the nose-cone off your original Bus gearbox and fit it to the Beetle unit. This will allow the gearbox to fit onto the original

mountings beneath the torsion tube, and to attach to the gear selector rod without a problem.

Put both gearboxes into the neutral position, before you undo the series of nuts around the nose-cone casing, as this makes life a lot easier. As the nose cone comes away, the thin paper gasket between the two mating surfaces will probably break, and must be replaced when fitting to the new unit. When the Bus nose cone is attached to the Beetle or Type 3 gearbox, make sure that the gear selector rod (popularly known as the 'hockey stick' due to its shape) is fitted into the gear selectors properly before tightening the casing down.

The next job is to exchange the original axle tubes on the Beetle or Type 3 with those from the kit. The axle nuts that hold the brake drums to the shafts will have to be loosened prior to the transmission being taken

High-grade copolymer axle gaiters (left) can be used to replace original rubber items (right), if required.

from the car. Then it is a matter of disassembling the brake drums and pulling the bearing from the axle shaft to allow removal of the axle tube. This process is very similar to that on the Bus, but just make a mental note of where everything goes, ready for reassembly. Six nuts secure the axle tube retainer at the gearbox end, which must be undone before the axle tube can be pulled off, together with the rubber gaiter and retainer plate. The paper gasket (or gaskets) behind the retainer plate can also be removed.

The axles, which are spade-ended and run in a socket type universal joint, will not be removed unless you are attempting to reuse the original Bus transmission, with new axles fitted. In this case, a strong circlip and thrust washer must be removed from the differential side gear to allow the axle to be withdrawn. The side gear and fulcrum plates should also be removed, as these are matched to the axles, and will need to be replaced with those

matching the new axle. For information on turning the differential around, a comprehensive VW workshop manual should be consulted.

The new axle tubes can now be slid into place using a new gasket (or gaskets), which give the spherical split plastic insert (sandwiched between the metal faces) the correct clearance of 0.008in (check this figure for the exact year of the gearbox you are using), with the plate nuts torqued to 14lb/ft. New rubber or stronger high-grade copolymer axle gaiters should also be used to prevent any possible oil leaks. If they're of the 'split design', put a little jointing compound on the mating faces of the sleeve as they are screwed together with the row of small nuts and bolts.

Do not fully tighten the nuts or affix the end metal clamping rings until the gearbox is refitted to the Bus, as the sleeve may otherwise twist (and subsequently split) when the vehicle is placed on the ground. Position the

sleeve so that the joint is not directly vertical at the top of the axle, as movement up and down will try to force it open. A position with the split set horizontal and facing to the rear is best.

With the new axle tube in place, refit the Beetle axle bearing (or a replacement) using a drift to locate it home. The brake drum and internal components can then be reassembled. One point worth noting is that if Beetle components are used, the brake drum will give a four-bolt wheel pattern. It's better to use the rear brake assembly from the pre-1965 Type 3 model (even if fitted to Beetle axles) since this gives you the earlier five-bolt wheel pattern (5 x 205mm), larger drums (248 x 46mm as opposed to 230 x 40mm on the later Beetles), and a 22.2mm wheel cylinder bore as standard. These drums are also the same dimension as the front drums on the 1300cc-engined 1302 and 1303 Beetles, which use a directly interchangeable wheel cylinder measuring 23.8mm - the largest VW Beetle cylinder produced - giving even better stopping power. Using earlier five-bolt Beetle drums and an additional spacer between the drum 'snout' and hub nut is possible, but not to be recommended, due to the narrower, brake shoe lining size.

SPRING PLATES

Fitting the new spring plates means removing the old ones, and this is a job that's time-consuming, but nothing to get overly concerned about. The spring plates are splined at the forward end to the torsion bars that run in the cylindrical tubes on each side of the Bus, just in front of the rear wheels. The two tempered steel bars provide the rear springing for the Transporter. They are splined at both ends, locking into a fixed collar at the centre, with the spring plates at the outer end.

They are also 'preloaded' with tension, which allows the suspension to absorb road shocks.

Adjustment of the height and camber at the rear of the Transporter can be achieved by rotating the spring plate, in relation to the torsion bar, by sliding it off the splines and refitting it in a different position. There are 48 splines at the outer end of the torsion bar, and 44 on the inner, so fine adjustments can be made by rotating the bar in one direction, and the spring plate in the other. If the torsion bar inner end is moved by one spline, the adjustment is altered by 8 deg 10′, and if the spring plate is moved one spline on the outer end of the bar the adjustment is 7 deg 35′. By moving the torsion bar one way, and the plate the other, fine adjustments to a minimum of 0 deg 40′ can be achieved.

I'm not prescribing you alter the height of the Transporter rear by this method, since the other modifications we're looking at adequately achieve this. It is important, however, to understand the principle in case a sagging torsion bar on one side needs correction, whilst the back end of the vehicle is receiving other work and could easily be accommodated. It should also be mentioned that the straight axle kit - whilst lowering the back of the Bus - won't entirely rid the suspension setup of the effects of positive camber (that is where the tyres are further apart at the top than the bottom) during driving, due simply to the nature of the swing axle design, without lowering the Bus a lot.

To achieve a more 'sensitive' tuning of the rear suspension height (and without radical lowering) an IRS conversion will be required, which will be covered later. It's also recommended to fit spring plate retaining straps around the spring plate during reassembly if you've

Spring plate retaining straps – here welded to a later model Bus – prevent the plates slipping off the bottom casting 'step'. (Courtesy Simon Glen)

lowered the Bus several inches, and are also running a high-performance engine. These bolt to the suspension casting (or can even be welded on), and prevent excessive downward movement of the rear suspension during acceleration, preventing the plates from slipping off the bottom casting 'step'.

Spring plate removal & replacement bushes

The spring plate can be removed from the outer end of the torsion bar by removing the four end cover bolts. Inevitably these won't have been removed before so be prepared to soak them in penetrating oil, or even use some heat from a small butane torch, to help loosen them before using a wrench. The rubber outer bushing

can be withdrawn and will be replaced. Chisel, or mark with paint, the position of the plate on the torsion bar and its level in relation to the metal casting behind it. The spring plate is still under considerable load-so be careful! The plate can then be carefully levered off the small step beneath it. Ensure your hands are well clear of the plate as it's released, as it will come down with considerable force. Don't allow it to dislodge the inner end of the torsion bar or this will create problems with realignment later. The inner rubber bush behind the plate will also be replaced.

The best performance items here are either brand new rubber VW items, or the inner and outer polyurethane (often called simply 'urethane') bushes supplied by Bluebird Customs or Red

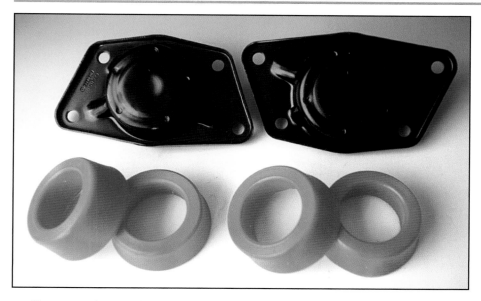

New VW rubber bump-stops.

New cover plates, and urethane inner and outer suspension bushes from Bluebird Customs.

9 Design. These specially formulated high-resilience elastomer bushes have exceptional mechanical properties and friction absorbing capabilities not attainable with rubber. The bushes are lighter than conventional rubber; don't break easily even in hard driving conditions; don't deteriorate or swell when in contact with grease, petrol or oil and are easy to fit, with a little grease or graphite. They have a high compression-bearing capability giving a 'tighter' feel to the suspension, whilst also eliminating unwanted vibration and noise in the same way as rubber bushes. They are also self-lubricating, with the bushes themselves releasing a microscopic amount of lubricating polymer during any movement, and are viable alternatives to 'original' VW rubber bushes during the rebuild. However, they are not to be recommended for IRS conversions as they are not flexible enough to allow correct flexion of the spring plates (see separate section).

The replacement spring plate should have some grease smeared onto the splined section and, with the new bushes in place, offered up to the end of the torsion bar in the same relationship as the original one. The plate will be hard to lever back up to its position resting on the small

suspension step. It is recommended that a trolley jack - with a chain running around it and fixed at the top shock absorber mounting to prevent the Bus from lifting - is used to carefully force the plate upwards. Once clear of the step it can be tapped with a soft-faced hammer until it's located on the torsion bar splines. Fitting the torsion bar end cap can also prove problematic, as the four bolts won't automatically line up. They could therefore damage the threads within the casting if they were forcibly wound

Rear urethane gearbox mounts are stronger than stock bonded rubber-and-metal items.

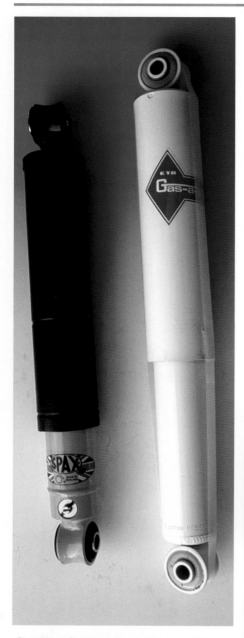

Gas-filled Spax shock absorbers (left) and KYB Gas-A-Just units (right).

manoeuvred into place for fitting, check the position of the rubber bump stop mountings on the old Transporter axle shaft. Make sure that the new shaft (with its separate bolt-on mounting and rubber cone) will put the stop in exactly the same position as before. If not, the mounts will need grinding off the old axle shafts, and welding to the new ones, with new rubbers fitted. An alternative method is to fabricate a new rubber cone mount from the rubber and metal mount, available as part of a standard Beetle front shock absorber mounting kit.

Finally, before fitting the new transaxle, change the gearbox mountings for either brand new rubber-and-metal bonded items or, preferably, urethane or even solid mounts. The later will give more interior noise within the Bus, but will never break. It will also allow the fitting of a padded transaxle strap around

the top of the gearbox for additional strength, if a high performance engine is to be added.

Fitting the new transaxle is then very much a reversal of the removal process with the new spring plates matching the mountings on the axle flanges of the new axle tubes. Only the toe-in/out adjustment will need accurate resetting, as mentioned before. Replacement shock absorbers are a must, and there are plenty to choose from. There are gas-filled Spax, and KYB Gas-A-Just units, as well as conventional oil-filled units, that work by channelling fluid through various valves to convert mechanical energy into heat thus dissipating it into the air. For the best ride, fit adjustable dampers with integral bump stops, as previously mentioned. Whichever you choose, check with your dealer that the size and damping function will be correct for your lowered Bus.

in. The best way is to use, diagonally, two longer bolts to locate the cap, whilst two short bolts are fitted. The two longer bolts can then be changed for the correct shorter items.

Before the new transaxle is

Lowering adds style ... Slammed and flamed Bus looks ready to cruise. (Courtesy Simon Glen)

LOWERED SPRING PLATES, ADJUSTABLE SPRING PLATES & BOOMERANG PLATES

Before detailing the Bus Independent Rear Suspension (IRS), let's take a look at the variety of spring plates and modification plates that are currently available. These can generally be used as 'stand alone' products or with the other modifications we're looking at.

We'll begin with straight and lowered spring plates. The straight spring plates from Red 9 Design are laser-cut steel items, for maximum

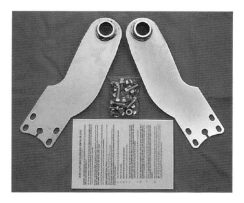

Red 9 Design 'lowered' spring plates replace VW items, or can be ordered 'straight' to fit a Beetle axle conversion. (Courtesy Red 9 Design)

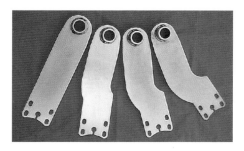

strength, and are basically straight replacements for the original VW items. Alternatively, they can be ordered shaped to fit to a Beetle axle tube, allowing a straight axle conversion. Generally, though, most buyers will want them with the raised rear section

to allow a lowered rear suspension, whilst maintaining standard ride quality and suspension travel. These allow the Bus to benefit from improved handling, with the reduced ride height, but without affecting the carrying capacity. Standard preload is maintained on the torsion bars, and there is the benefit of the Bus having a lowered centre of gravity for better cornering, and increased static positive camber.

Since they come in either 2in, 3in or 4in dropped designs, they can give different rear heights without resorting to turning the original VW spring plates on the torsion bar splines. This tends to make the rear too soft compared to the front suspension, and allows pitching over bumps and cornering instability. For a reduction gearbox-type Transporter more than a 2in drop should not be considered, but for straight axle and IRS designs they provide additional lowering options. Since they also work with standard shock absorbers rather than shorter or uprated items, they provide a low cost way of dropping the Bus rear. The Red 9 Design plates are available in early (up to mid-1971) or late (mid- 1971 onwards) spline sizes.

Fitting lowered spring plates
Fitting them follows the process described earlier for removing and replacing the VW spring plates, but it's worth noting the following points to ensure accurate setting of the plates. When fitting the original spring plate to a Bus, which still has its original factory rear suspension setting, mark its place in its unloaded position on to the chassis member behind. This will be the same position at which the new plate requires fitting. If the original setting has been altered already, then obtaining the correct preload for the lowered spring plate is trickier, but not impossible.

The plate should be fitted to the torsion bar with the upper edge, closest to the spline, at an angle of 17 deg to 20 deg relative to the door sill (swing axle Buses). To achieve this use a protractor and spirit level to take a measurement along the bottom of the door sill. Next calculate the angle at which the spring plate needs to be fitted (and you should refer to a competent workshop manual for your year of Bus for this) and locate the plate to the torsion bar. For IRS spring plates, take the measurement from the lower edge of the plate. With the lowered spring plate set at the correct angle and with the raised rear section uppermost, put the bushing back in place before fitting the cover plate. If you're using original rubber bushes, make sure that the word 'oben' is at the top, as this is the way VW designed the bush. Using some talcum powder on the bushes aids free movement and prevents 'squeaks'.

ADJUSTABLE SPRING PLATES
There are many other versions of the stepped spring plate, but other spring plates are also made in adjustable designs. They have one considerable advantage over non-adjustable spring plates, whether stepped or not, in that they allow you to reset the rear suspension without continually disassembling the spring

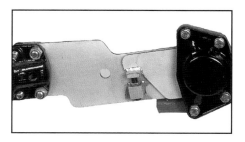

Creative Engineering adjustable spring plates. (Courtesy Creative Engineering)

**Creative Engineering spacers.
(Courtesy Creative Engineering)**

plates from the torsion bars, axle tubes or IRS A-arms. Their main disadvantage is price, though some might argue that the Bus will also suffer from reduced suspension travel, and that they are ultimately weaker

**Indian Automotive adjustable spring plate.
(Courtesy Simon Glen)**

**Custom Bugs & Buses adjustable spring plate and rear disc brake conversion for T2 transporter, with floating caliper.
(Courtesy Simon Glen)**

than a one-piece design. However, they're part of the total suspension kit supplied by companies such as Creative Engineering in the UK, Indian Automotive and Custom Bugs and Buses in Australia, and are all manufactured to the highest quality.

Whilst Creative Engineering's plates are specifically supplied for the Bus IRS Conversion using stepped spring plates, and Custom Bugs and Buses design is for a straight plate as part of a disc brake conversion kit,

**Close-up of adjustable spring plate fitted to rear suspension.
(Courtesy Simon Glen)**

Indian Automotive makes adjustable plates in both designs. As with most things in the performance parts' market, 'you pays your money and takes your choice', and you will need to carefully select the version that best suits your requirements and budget.

The final conversion in this section is the addition of what are known as 'boomerang plates' (so called because of their shape) to the Bus IRS suspension. Manufactured by Bus Boys, these plates are designed to fit between the hub carrier and the spring plate, thereby lowering the Bus by 3in - 4in, without any detriment to the camber settings of the vehicle. These are purely bolt-on parts, and

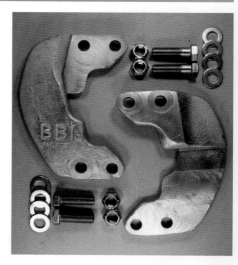

Bus Boys 'Boomerang Plates' – so called due to their shape.

easy to fit without major modifications to the rest of the suspension. Similar plates are also offered by Custom Bugs and Buses in Australia, and use an additional strengthening bar between the plate and diagonal A-arm for extra reinforcement.

INDEPENDENT REAR SUSPENSION (IRS) CONVERSION
One of the most popular rear

Custom Bugs & Buses lowering plates use a strengthening bar for additional reinforcement. (Courtesy Simon Glen)

suspension conversions on an early Split-screen Bus is fitting an Independent Rear Suspension (IRS). For some, it simply removes the reduction box type transmission, and lowers the back of the Bus for aesthetic looks. Whilst for others it's a way of providing a more 'modern' suspension system similar to the later Bay-window Bus design, and gives better fuel consumption, better acceleration and better cruising speeds. Either way, it offers more tuning possibilities than the earlier swing axle design. There

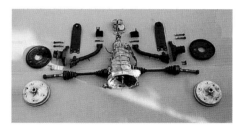

Volksheaven IRS conversion kit for Buses. (Courtesy Volksheaven)

are now a number of companies offering conversion kits, and we'll take a look at the best known on the market and what's involved in making the conversion, before detailing the installation of one of the kits.

The IRS kit from UK company Volksheaven is one of the most economic of the kits on the market, simply because it uses mostly stock VW parts sourced from other donor vehicles. All the parts can be supplied together as a kit, or individually. The kit comes with a gearbox from a 1600cc Beetle (the 1302s or 1303s 'Super Beetle'), though any IRS Beetle gearbox can be used, providing you ensure that the gearbox final drive ratio will optimise the performance of the engine you've chosen to fit. The gearbox nose cone comes from the original Split-screen Bus (1958-1967).

All the brakes, hubs, driveshafts, stub axles, spring plates and trailing

Easi-Lo IRS Bus brackets have to be shaped to fit the torsion tubes, and provide mountings for the Beetle diagonal A-arms.

arms are those from a 1968-1969 'big' five stud brake drum Transporter (five bolt x 205mm), whilst the hand brake cables and conduits are from a later T25 van. The diagonal A-arms are shortened items from a 1970s Bay-window Bus - this modification is necessary for the A-arms to miss the two frame horns that the gearbox bolts to. Note that earlier Bay arms are a different shape and need more cutting to make them fit, so do not use these. The mounting brackets that pivot the A-arms at the torsion bar tube end are cut from a Bay-window Bus, and must be removed accurately. An alternative to using brackets cut from another van

is to use specially made Easi-Lo IRS Bus brackets made by Classic-Leisure & Commercial, though they still have to be shaped to fit the torsion tubes.

Finally, you will need two CV joint assemblies from the IRS Beetle to attach the gearbox to the Bus driveshafts. Since the Beetle CVs are narrower than the Bus items, you will need some strong, snug-fitting circlips to fit up against the inner shoulder of the driveshaft before fitting the CV joint, so that the end circlip holds them firmly on to the Bus shafts without any movement.

Proving the interchangeability of VW components you can consider using the stronger Bus CVs on the inner end of the driveshafts to ensure longevity. The larger diameter (100mm) Bay-window Bus or Type 4 (411 or 412) models use a more durable CV than a Beetle item, and are to be favoured. The Bus joint is the same diameter as the Type 4 unit, but is deeper, at 35mm, thus allowing extra movement. It can operate at angles up to 19 deg intermittently and 17 deg on a continuous basis.

These joints can be supplied by

Bus CV joints, new axle boots, and VW 181 gearbox drive flanges.

The 'big' 5-bolt pattern brake drums will be lost during an IRS conversion. This is an early (1955-1963) drum. (Courtesy Custom & Speed Parts)

Internals of fully rebuilt Bay-window transporter rear drum. (Courtesy Paul Knight)

Porsche parts, since the Porsche 924 and early 944 (pre-1986) use the same CVs as the Bay-window Bus and Type 4. Using these modifications, you get the stronger CVs at both ends. We will look at Porsche conversions later.

Before we give some technical advice on the installation, here's one final thought. Since the removal of the reduction boxes will mean your engine will rev lower, the braking effect of the engine will be less, and more pedal power will be required to apply the brakes, if you have drums all round. If you don't mind losing the earlier 'big' 5-stud pattern brake drum at the back, you can opt to change to the late Bay-window Bus 'small' - PCD pattern drums (five-bolt x 112mm), back

companies like Volksheaven (new or second-hand), but there is still the problem of how to mate them to

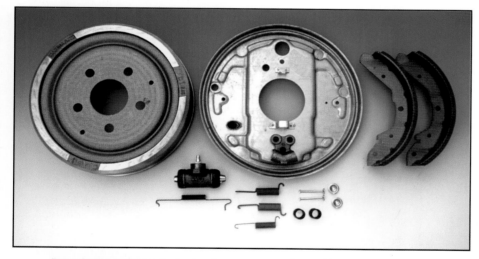

Bay-window transporter brake drum components, and 'small' 5-bolt drums.

the Beetle gearbox. VW themselves provided the answer with the gearbox drive flanges fitted to the later VW 181 (Thing/Trekker) model as these will accommodate the CV joints at the inner end. These IRS flanges are easily removed by prising out a centre cap and removing a retaining circlip, before replacing them with the 181 flanges. These are still available from VW dealers. It is also possible to use

plates, stub-axles and internals to allow better braking.

You will still need to use the early Bay spring plates, but you will end up with a stud pattern that matches a front disc brake assembly added to a '68 - 69 ball-joint front suspension, if you have made this conversion at the front. This will keep the stud pattern uniform and it allows a greater choice of modern wheels. The alloy wheels

from a Mercedes, Audi or Ford will fit straight on, for example.

Fitting these components requires a fair amount of work, some welding, and general help with moving heavy components around. It is not a 'Bolt-On' affair, though we'll look at those next.

As a matter of routine, it's always best to loosen the large axle nuts on the end of the driveshafts before jacking up a Bus to do any

Many modern alloy wheels are a bolt-on affair with the Bay-window drum PCD pattern. (Courtesy Paul Knight)

**Split-screen Bus with original swing axle transmission awaiting conversion.
(Courtesy Paul Utting)**

We've covered the removal process of the reduction box transmission before, so there's no need to detail it here. When the 'new' gearbox is offered into place make sure that the rear gearbox mounts (the ones that seat in the transmission cradle under the gearbox) are replaced by either new or urethane mounts, as they are liable to wear and could otherwise lead to problems. The starter motor and the clutch cable can be fitted at this point. Check that the clutch throw-out bearing in the bell-housing of the gearbox is compatible with the clutch you have fitted to your engine. There are various types of clutch-spring or diaphragm-and differences according to year. The spring type meets the release bearing via three large actuating arms, whilst the later diaphragm type has a multi-finger design, which the release bearing pushes against whilst moving on a guide tube.

The next job is to replace the original Split-screen Bus spring plates with those from the 1968 - 1969 Bay window. We have looked at the process of spring plate removal before, but just remember to mark the position of the original plates once they are released from the small metal step on the suspension casting. This allows the replacement plate to be fitted to the torsion bar at exactly the same angle. Do not remove or dislodge the torsion bar from its position on the inner set of splines, or this will cause real problems with resetting the rear suspension.

Once the new spring plates are mounted, and raised back on to the step, the modified A-arms will need to be offered up to the plates. The arms will have been shortened near the point where they attach to the spring plates, and the curve of the arms changed where they mount to the brackets on the torsion tube. Before fully bolting them up to the spring

transmission work, as you won't have the opportunity to undo them later. Also, check to make sure that the parts you're buying also have the axle nuts loosened, or you might have to chisel them off. This risks damage to the stub axle threads. The Bus can then be jacked up, and placed securely on axle stands, before removing the wheels, disconnecting the battery, removing the engine, and draining the oil from the old transaxle to avoid spillage later.

Fitting an IRS suspension
The gearbox should be set in the neutral position before removing the transmission, as should the gearbox that will replace it. Since the nose cone of the original gearbox will be fitted to the replacement gearbox, this makes it easier to ensure the correct engagement of the 'hockey stick' in the gear selectors when the swap is made. You need to use the original nose cone to get the gearbox to fit the mount attached to the torsion bar tube.

The bonded rubber and metal mount should be checked and replaced for a new one, or a urethane replacement as a matter of course. A new paper gasket will be needed between the nose cone and the main gearbox, so make sure you have one handy when you make the swap.

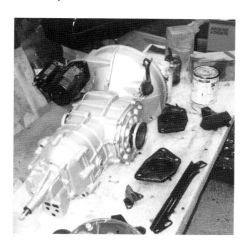

**Beetle 1303 IRS gearbox ready to be fitted to early Bus. Starter motor is attached.
(Courtesy Paul Utting)**

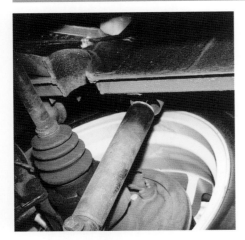

Chassis channelled to clear IRS axles for road use – here shown on a 1971 Crew Cab Bus. (Courtesy Simon Glen)

A-arms fitted and drums in place on Split Screen van. (Courtesy Paul Utting)

everything for fit. There may be a slight clearance problem between the arms as they move upwards, and the rear cradle This may need modification to relieve it.

With the wheels back on the Bus, but with it still jacked up, set all the components as near to the measurements you took before removing components from the donor Bay-window Bus (or to the specifications of the supplier). Set a small amount of positive camber, since the Bus will squat down slightly at the back when set on the floor. You will now need to tack weld the brackets in place, so lower the van down and see if it sits correctly. A tracking gauge will help here, if you have one. It is possible to make small adjustments to the settings by inserting shims between the spring plate and axle housings, but this isn't recommended as it will weaken the design. If the settings are wrong, the tack welds will have to be ground down, and the process

plates and stub axle housings, clean a section on each side of the torsion bar tube with a grinder at the place where the arm brackets will have to be welded on. Bolt the mounts that were cut from a donor Bay-window Bus up to the A-arms, put the stub axles and drums back in place, and check

repeated. If you wish, you can weld the brackets to a curved plate that can be clamped around the torsion tube and adjusted without tacking until the correct position has been found. It may take many attempts to get the settings correct, so take plenty of time and get it right.

When everything is aligned, take the A-arms off, and fully weld the mounts to the torsion tube. If you don't feel competent to weld (or don't have the equipment), get a specialist to help, as this is the most important part of the operation, and the brackets must stay on! Once the mounts are fitted, the A-arms can go back on, and the driveshafts and CVs can be attached. If the rubber CV boots look suspect, then

Trial fit of all IRS components into early Bus before welding brackets in place. (Courtesy Paul Utting)

Replacement CV joint boots are available in stronger coloured copolymer, or original rubber design, to replace any split items.

replace them with new or copolymer ones for longevity.

The brake assemblies can be rebuilt at this stage, using new brake cylinders, shoes and brake pipes as necessary. The flexible brake pipe will need to be attached to the mount on the A-arm, so the

Handbrake cables and outer conduits from a T3 (T25) van are needed to complete the IRS conversion. This T3 Caravelle has a rear disc brake conversion by Shermans Volks Conversions.
(Courtesy Simon Glen)

mount will need to be relocated unless longer pipes are used. Teflon coated or stainless braided brake lines from Bluebird Customs are the best possible replacements for high performance, plus they look good too! Using handbrake cables and outer conduits from a T25 van gets round any problems with cable lengths.

On T1 and T2 transporters, the rear shock absorbers are merely bolted at the top into a captive nut in the side frame bracket. A stronger mount is provided by welding on a new 'U' – shaped bracket to the frame to prevent the bolt flexing.
(Courtesy Simon Glen)

The original outer conduits could be adapted, though, by adding a spacer between the end of the outer cable and back plate.

The final modification is to the rear shock absorber top mounts. To strengthen the weak mountings for the bolts that run through the eye of the shock absorber into captive nuts in the side frame brackets, new 'U' shaped brackets can be welded onto the body, effectively surrounding the head of the shock absorber. The bracket-made of a 30mm long piece of channel section

steel with a hole in it for the bolt to pass through-will provide additional strength to the mounting, and prevent the shock absorber locating bolt from flexing and even shearing off altogether if heavily stressed.

Following your conversion, the choice of shock absorbers is yours, but you will need to take into account the height difference. Stock units from the front of a late Bay window Bus will fit, but there are a whole plethora of performance aftermarket units available. Spax units, and KYB Gas-A-Just being just two of the designs on the market. With new oil in the gearbox, the engine refitted, the brakes bled and adjusted, and all mounting nuts and bolts re-checked, the Bus is ready to roll.

Other IRS conversions & kits

A variation of the above conversion is to fit a larger proportion of Beetle parts, including the diagonal A-arms, brake drums and driveshafts. This type of conversion would require the A-arm mounts salvaged from a scrap IRS Beetle (or new aftermarket equivalents) and would follow much the same process to install.

A commercially available kit from Harry Harpics follows this principle, but instead of a welded A-arm mount, uses a bolt-on clamp to allow easier setting of track and camber. The clamp has only one set of bolts per side, allowing the clamp to hinge open on a silver steel pin, thus avoiding the heater tubes that run close to the mounting. The Bus spring plates are modified to fit to the Beetle A-arms where they bolt together, making the conversion a cost-effective alternative to using a mix of Bay window Bus and Beetle parts. It also allows a conversion back to the earlier style of transmission if it is later required.

By principally using Beetle

Harry Harpic's bolt-on IRS conversion for Buses also allows the fitting of Porsche brakes.

parts, a further upgrade option of using Beetle aftermarket rear disc brake kits, or Porsche components, becomes available. Beetle rear disc brake conversions are covered in the book 'How to modify Beetle suspension, brakes and chassis for high performance', so they won't be detailed here.

It is worth noting that Harry Harpics conversion kit is aimed at allowing the whole diagonal A-arm assembly, hubs, stub axles and rear disc brakes from a Porsche 924 or early 944 (pre-1986) to be transplanted into the Split screen Bus. The main visible difference between the Beetle stub axles and those on the Porsche 924/944 (which use the same length and spline arrangement as the Beetle), are the larger drive flanges to accommodate the larger Porsche CV joints. The joints are the same diameter as the Bay-window Bus and Type 4 (411 or 412) units and, like the Bus items, are more durable than stock Beetle CVs. So, with a choice of stronger CVs they can be mounted to the Bay-window driveshafts (but not

ones from an automatic). They will also fit the Porsche stub axles at the outer ends, and VW 181 (Trekker/Thing) drive flanges at the inner gearbox end. This provides the correct overall length of axle shaft and joints to fit between the 181 output flanges and the Porsche stub-axles. Always check driveshaft lengths before any modification, as some shafts (both VW and Porsche) do vary. The resultant combination of parts must not allow any movement of

the joints on the shaft. Other Porsche conversions using 5-speed gearboxes and Porsche Turbo 930/935 CV joints are outside the scope of this book-but are possible!

In much the same style as the 'bolt-on' conversion above, are those by Wolfgang International and Bus Boys in the US, and Custom & Speed Parts in Germany. These conversion kits come with the control arm (A-arm) bolt-on mounting brackets, special spring plates, and correct length axles for the IRS switchover. The parts needed from a donor VW are the A-arms, brake drum assemblies, stub axles, CV joints, transmission and nuts and bolts. The parts can be sourced from any IRS Beetle, Type 3 (Notchback/Squareback/ Fastback) or 181 Thing/Trekker. The Beetle and Type 3 parts will lower the rear end as we've already seen, but the 181 parts will keep it at stock height (the vehicle originally came with a reduction box transaxle, and the IRS version was designed to maintain the same ground clearance at the back).

Installation of these kits follows the same basic procedure though - since the driveshafts are provided in the kit - it is better to stay with the

Custom & Speed Parts bolt-on IRS conversion for Buses. This kit includes special spring plates and correct length axles. (Courtesy Custom & Speed Parts)

recommended Beetle CVs unless you wish to modify Bay-window Bus units to fit. This can be achieved, however, by machining the inner face of the Bus CV joint so that it allows the wider joint to sit further on to the shorter axle shaft, allowing the spring clip to be added. Note that modifying the shoulder of any driveshaft by machining it down (where the CV abuts the axle shaft shoulder to allow it to fully slide onto the splines) cannot be recommended, as it considerably weakens the shaft.

KRUIZINWAGON IRS KIT

Certainly one of the most innovative and well-developed 'Bolt-on' IRS conversion kit is that supplied by Indian Automotive in Australia, under their Kruizinwagon brand. Their IRS conversion kit uses an adjustable bolt-on control arm mount clamped to the torsion bar tube, similar to other kits, but with many other refinements. The clamp can be fitted using hand tools, so there is no cutting or welding required to fit the kit into a Split-screen Bus. The clamp houses a large eccentric bushing to mount the control arm, which allows extra adjustment

Underside of the Kruizinwagon IRS conversion, with control arm and clamp fitted. This kit can be fitted with hand tools. (Courtesy Simon Glen)

A large eccentric bushing is fitted at the clamp, and this can be used to set wheel alignment. (Courtesy Simon Glen)

for the arms. This is important, as the lower a Bus is dropped at the rear, the worse the rear wheel alignment becomes. This is normally difficult to correct, but this system aids proper alignment. This same clamp and bushing can be used in Bay-window Buses, providing the factory mount is removed first, and allows the rear to be dropped low.

The rear control arms are also adjustable in two planes. The spring plates to which they mount are adjustable on a threaded bolt for vertical movement, and via 10mm thick drop plates (similar to Boomerang plates) for lateral movement to adjust camber and toe setting. The drop plate gives a $3^{1}/_{2}$in drop instantly, but ride quality is maintained by adding a bump stop in a mount, located where the original shock absorber mount was positioned. The shock absorber attaches to a new mount located further back on the rear suspension member.

To pass the stringent Australian construction laws all Kruizinwagon products are tested for over 30,000km with regular checks every 10km before being made available for general purchase. The net result is a product that is user friendly, and robust. On the Split-screen van, the conversion can also be reversed, if ever required.

A thick drop plate allows lateral adjustment of the suspension, whilst the adjustable spring plate gives height adjustment. (Courtesy Simon Glen)

Indian Automotive also specialise in lowering and raising Bay-window Buses, and have perfected chassis channelling to allow driveshaft clearance on lowered Buses for road use.

CREATIVE ENGINEERING BEETLE-TO-BUS IRS FITTING

Probably one of the best engineered IRS conversion kits available in Europe is supplied by Creative Engineering. The kit has been developed by years of research into ways of improving the Bus's rear suspension design, whilst retaining as many of the original VW parts as possible, and following VW inbuilt engineering principles. Whilst the VW rear suspension is very simple and effective, it is rather crude in the way it works. It depends greatly on

A new bump-stop mount bolts into the old shock absorber mount. The damper mount is moved to a new position. (Courtesy Simon Glen)

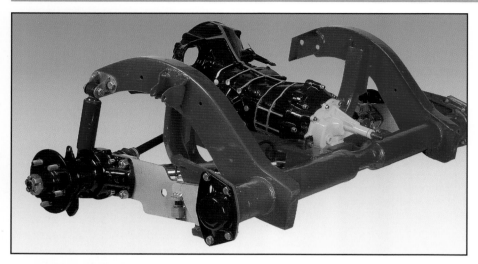

Creative Engineering Beetle to Bus IRS conversion kit has been developed after years of research to use as many VW parts as possible. (Courtesy Creative Engineering)

both the material that the spring plates are made from (tensile steel), and the two rubber bushes ('doughnuts') located at the torsion bar end of the spring plate where it attaches to the torsion bar. These allow the flex in the spring plate to be absorbed when the suspension moves. The plate is acting as a spring (hence 'spring plate') and won't fatigue and snap, as it would if it was made of mild steel. VW calculated the ride height and weight carrying capacity of the Bus, but never allowed for others to start modifying it!

The earliest known way of lowering a Bus (or Beetle) was to slide the spring plate off the torsion bar and relocate it on another spline. Since the design uses 48 splines at the outer end (the inner end has 44), there is plenty of opportunity for fine adjustment of the rear suspension. If you divide the 360 deg of the torsion bar by the 48 splines, you find that each spline gives 7 deg 5´ adjustment (the inner works out at 8 deg 1´), so the difference between the two is a minimal 0 deg 68´. Moving the spring plate one way on the outer splines, and moving the torsion bar on the inner splines within

the housing, allows fine adjustment. However, many early Bus customisers simply relocated the spring plate one spline on the torsion bars to give a 3in drop. This increased the camber at the rear (the wheels will be pointing in at the top), giving the effect of a van full of heavy commercial goods. The loading that VW had carefully calculated was suddenly used up - loading on all the joints and bearings increased, with tyres starting to wear unevenly.

Drop the Bus any further (even one more spline) and more serious problems occur. The live axle will be completely overloaded, the increase in negative camber will cause the spring plate to twist beyond its limit, and the shock absorbers (even shorter ones) will bottom out, which creates a terrible ride, and ultimately destroys the units. The suspension components fighting each other is bad enough, but it also means that you can't remove your rear wheel without two jacks-one to lift the wheel, and one to force the spring plate down. Fitting adjustable spring plates helps, but it is not a good setup for the Bus itself, or the driver.

You now need to consider what happens to the control arm operation when the previous swing axle design of the Split-screen Bus becomes an IRS system. Whilst the axle swings in one arc, and the spring plate swings with it at approximately 90 deg , the control arm will be fixed to a mount positioned on the torsion bar tube. It will then be swinging in a smaller arc than the spring plate. When the arm is bolted to the spring plate at the hub end it is then fixed and becomes an A-arm with the spring plate.

Since the assembly now has to operate in different arcs, it can only continue to swing and work because of the flexion in the rubber bushes at the torsion bar end, and at the control arm pivot point. The ideal is to keep these as flexible rubber bushes, though it is appreciated that a new control arm bush is no longer available from VW, and therefore a urethane replacement may have to be considered (such as a Superflex bush). The torsion bar 'doughnut' rubber bushes, however, should be replaced only with new VW rubber bushes. Urethane bushes here are not flexible enough, and will cause a failure elsewhere in the system.

The most common problem will be that suspension loads will be transferred to the hub, and movement will occur at the slotted adjustment holes in the spring plates until they wear into an oval shape, no matter how tightly the bolts are torqued up. The golden rule on an IRS suspension system is to avoid urethane and stick with rubber. The exceptions are the front or rear gearbox mounts, where urethane replacements are acceptable.

Fitting the Creative Engineering IRS kit
Enough of the theory, now let's look at the parts needed to complete this IRS conversion and what comes in Creative

Engineering's kit. First and foremost from your original Split-screen Bus you will need to retain the two torsion bars. Simply leave them in place, and do not move them as you don't want to lose the original VW factory setting. You will also need to keep the original gearbox nose cone and 'hockey stick', as we've seen with other conversions. The front gearbox mount can also be reused if it is in good condition, but it is worth changing this for a brand new bonded rubber and metal VW item, or a urethane replacement.

From a Beetle (or IRS Type 3), you will need the IRS gearbox, 2 CV joints to mate to the Beetle gearbox output flanges (though you can use the stronger IRS Bus items and the VW 181 output flanges), and a pair of Beetle rear shock absorbers if you are lowering the Bus between 3in - 5in (the mountings are the same as the Bus, but the units are shorter). Alternatively, aftermarket shock absorbers are available for this conversion.

From a Bay-window Bus, you'll

Bus gearbox nose cone is used on Beetle IRS gearbox. Urethane front mount is stronger than a bonded metal and rubber item. (Courtesy Creative Engineering)

**Detail of outer CV joint attached to Bus hub. Control arm mounting can be seen behind driveshaft.
(Courtesy Creative Engineering)**

need the complete hub assemblies, which should be from the 1968 - 1969 model year if you still wish to retain the large five-bolt x 205mm PCD bolt pattern, or from 1970 onwards if you prefer the five-bolt x 112mm PCD bolt pattern. If only the later pattern is available (the earlier ones are becoming rarer), companies such as Machine 7 sell billet adaptors to allow the fitting of 205mm wheels to the later bolt pattern, as well as adaptors to fit Porsche pattern (five-bolt x 130mm PCD) or any other five bolt pattern to the later hubs. So if you fancy a five-bolt Mercedes pattern to match the Mercedes 190 discs you've had re-drilled with a five-bolt 100mm PCD pattern at the front, then it is probably better to use these parts anyway. You'll also need the Bay-window driveshafts which can be from any year Bus - as long as they are not from an automatic model as they are shorter-plus the Bus CV joints.

You will also need to source

spring plates, and there are two options. Either find a pair of the 1968 - 1969 Bay-window ones (which are getting hard to find), or purchase Creative Engineering's own adjustable replacements. These are ready 'stepped' (so they allow a certain lowering of the rear suspension anyway), plus they allow the suspension to be adjusted without disassembling the parts later, and are a worthwhile investment.

The other parts you will need are the pair of control arms (A-arms), again from a 1968 - 1969 Bay-window Bus. The originals are certainly strong items - having a 3.5mm thick wall, and a forging where the arm meets the hub plate - but they will need the flexible brake pipe mounts relocated to the top of the arm for better access. They are also getting hard to find, but do not be tempted to use two from the same side of a Bus, and swap one over to the other side. They look the same but they are 'handed', and can only be used in the one position without altering suspension geometry. The alternative is to use Creative's

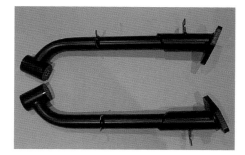

**Creative Engineering control arm replaces hard to find 1968-1969 Bay-window Bus arms for this conversion.
(Courtesy Creative Engineering)**

own control arms, which are 4mm CDS (Cold Drawn Seamless steel) with reinforcement at the hub attachment, and the brake pipe mounts ready relocated. The other prerequisites

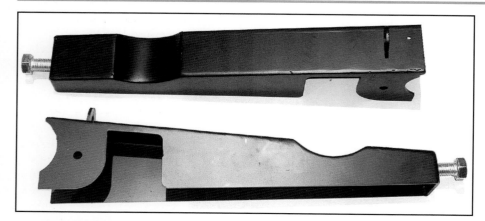

Replacement chassis legs are Creative Engineering items, designed to allow full movement of the driveshafts and control arms. (Courtesy Creative Engineering)

for this conversion are the two IRS replacement chassis legs and the two shock absorber mountings, which Creative Engineering supply.

Installation

The installation process begins in much the same way as other conversions we've covered. Firstly the battery must be disconnected before the engine is removed. The reduction gearbox transaxle must also be removed, as must the spring plates and rubber bushes, without dislodging the torsion bars themselves. In the engine bay, the

New shock absorber mountings that are fitted to the rear section of the chassis. (Courtesy Creative Engineering)

fuel tank will now be clearly visible, as it sits in a position behind the engine. This must now be completely drained, and the tank removed. Once emptied, it may appear tempting to leave it in situ but remember it is the vapour given off by petrol that is explosive, and it will only take one spark from your welding (and there will be a lot of them!) to ignite it. Place the empty tank well away from the area in which you will be working-preferably even out of the building.

You will now be removing the two original rear frame forks that supported the swing axle gearbox, as they will be entirely replaced. You will need an angle grinder, a hacksaw, and safety equipment, including goggles, strong gloves and ear defenders. Remove the rear part of the forks with the first hacksaw cuts, then cut the other side of the 'U' support cradle to release it from the forks (see diagram 1). Finally cut off the remaining part of the forks as close to the torsion bar tube as possible. You now have access with a small grinder to clean up any remaining edges on both the torsion bar housing, and the support cradle. The cradle will still be located by the upper part of the chassis rear. Now you will need your ear defenders! Do

not grind away any more material than necessary. Finish off by sanding the torsion tube, and the flat top of the channel support, with a 60-grit sanding disc to ensure a clean surface on which to weld, as good weld penetration will be critical.

The two new IRS replacement chassis legs will now be fitted. Refer to diagram 2 to understand the measurements you will need to fix these accurately in place. Begin by bolting a transmission cross member (either a stock or a reinforced aftermarket gearbox cradle) on to the ends of the two replacement IRS chassis legs using the two large 20mm bolts supplied. Ensure the side cutouts (where the control arms will need to clear the chassis legs as they rise) are facing outwards and with the aperture downwards. With the cradle bolted across the ends, the correct rear spacing of 300mm is ensured.

The most important measurement to get right is that from A - B, which is 215mm, and this is measured from a centre line marked on the torsion bar housing - remember the old carpenter's rule: measure twice! By using the gearbox cradle and these measurements, the chassis legs can only be fitted in one place. These measurements will allow the chassis legs to abut the torsion bar housing so that they are vertical, parallel and square to it before you tack-weld them onto the tube, and the support cradle. Check the measurements again and, if everything is perfectly lined up, weld the legs to the torsion tube housing, and the support cradle. Once they have cooled off, apply a rust-inhibiting paint for protection, and a top coat to enhance your Bus's looks and improve its weather resistance.

Now the parts from other VW donor vehicles can be fitted. Begin by replacing the gearbox nose cone and

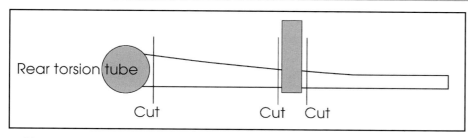

Diagram 1. The rear part of the original chassis forks will be cut away, leaving the 'U' – support cradle. (Courtesy Creative Engineering).

hockey stick with the one off your old Split-screen Bus transmission, and seat it with a new gasket. Fit the gearbox to the rear gearbox cradle using new bonded metal and rubber mounts or urethane replacements, and a new mount at the front. It's a good idea to also change the gearbox oil at this point whilst access is relatively easy, and to check the condition of the gearbox oil seal around the output shaft, the throw-out bearing and the retaining clips for the bearing. Make sure that the throw out bearing will also match the clutch pressure plate you have fitted to your engine before you attempt to mate the two together.

Now fit the control arms into their position within the chassis legs, and bolt them in using the M12 bolts and lock nut provided in the kit. Do not over-tighten these bolts, as you should be able to move the arms up and down by hand. The locknuts, once on, should be replaced if they are ever undone, as they are designed to only be used once. Remember to get the arms fitted to the correct sides, with the brake pipe bracket at the top of the arm. If you are using the Creative Engineering replacement arms, the right one is stamped 'R' (the left one is unstamped) on the bottom of the hub mounting flange. This assumes you are looking at the assembly from the back.

With the transmission mounted, you can now fit the driveshafts and CV joints. If you use Beetle CVs at the gearbox end, you will also need to put one (or two) spacer washers between the CV and the retaining circlip, and these are supplied with Creative's kit. This is due to the Beetle CV being slightly narrower than the Bus equivalent, and the spacer (or spacers, depending on the make of CV used, as they differ) takes up any movement of the CV on the splines of the shaft. The CVs will, of course, move in and out slightly as they move with the arc of the axle. This is due to the design of the joint, with its ball bearings located between inner and outer races. This is the beauty of the IRS ('double-joint') system. It allows the driveshafts (axles) longitudinal movement in and out of the joints to accommodate rear suspension travel and provide optimum handling without adverse camber or toe changes. The position of all the parts is shown in the diagram 3. If you prefer to use Bus CVs, then the gearbox drive flanges should be changed for VW 181 units to accommodate them.

The next parts to be installed are the spring plates, which can either be Bay-window Bus items (1968 - 1969), or the Creative Engineering adjustable items. If you can find them, the former may be cheaper, but they don't offer

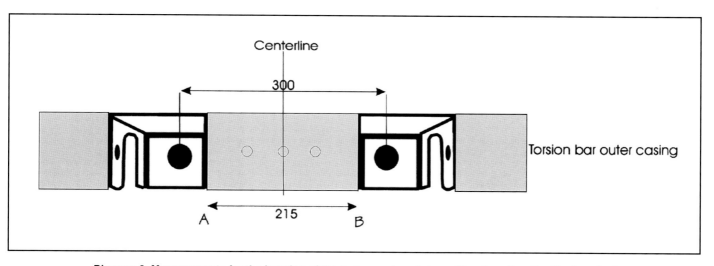

Diagram 2. Measurements for the location of the two new chassis legs. (Courtesy Creative Engineering)

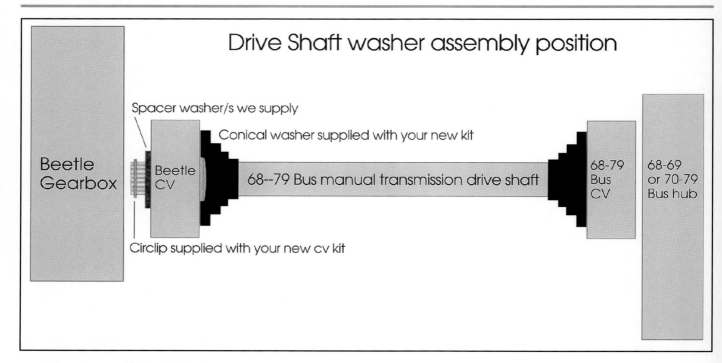

Diagram 3. Positioning of all the components on the driveshaft. (Courtesy Creative Engineering)

the opportunity for fine adjustment like the latter, so be prepared for more trial and error fitting until you have established the correct ride height (see diagram 4). In either case, fit new VW rubber 'doughnut' bushes, and make sure the two plates are set at the same height. Accurate measuring will be needed to confirm this.

The spring plate covers can now be re-attached (new ones looks good). If you choose to fit the adjustable spring plates, you'll need to use the thin metal spacers provided behind the covers but do not fully tighten the covers down - leave them loose enough for you to slightly move the plate up or down. When fitted, the spring plates should line up with the mounting face at the end of the control arm, and there should be little or no gap between the two items. More importantly, the spring plate should mate to the control arm mounting face without twisting.

With the spring plates installed and lining up with the control arms, the hub assemblies can now be offered up, and loosely held in place with the four M14 bolts that locate them at each

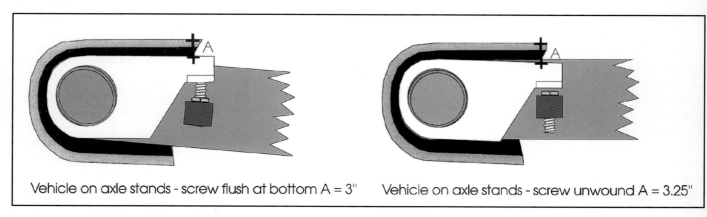

Diagram 4. Establishing the correct ride height of the spring plates. (Courtesy Creative Engineering)

side of the Bus. Ensure that you put the two fine threaded bolts into the tapped holes in the hub, and the other two coarse pitch bolts through the unthreaded hub holes. If a bolt doesn't fit immediately don't force it, as you could damage the thread-try another. Do not fully tighten the bolts down for a moment.

The rear shock absorbers need to be fitted next, and you will have to bolt the new shock absorber mounts to the rear of the chassis, making sure that you fit large washers to the inside of the chassis to spread the load. The choice of shock absorbers is yours, but allow approximately 100mm of travel when the Bus is on the ground. For most Buses that have been lowered approximately 3in, the use of a Beetle rear shock absorber is recommended. These are shorter than the stock Bus unit, and will not bottom out. If you are planning on lowering the Bus more than this, you will have to consider extending the lower shock absorber mount to prevent the unit bottoming out and being damaged. You may also consider aftermarket performance shock absorbers. These are fine providing that you end up with about 100mm of travel (see diagram 5).

When you are happy that everything is perfectly lined up, put the Bus back on its wheels, so it is resting with its full weight on the suspension parts. Only now should everything be fully tightened up. Some slight adjustment to the toe in/out settings can be made by moving the hub front to back on the slotted spring plate holes. You will need to consult a VW workshop manual for setting instructions. Whilst there will be some affect on camber due to the lowering of the Bus, the CVs will generally compensate for this, and will not create the problems normally associated with lowering a live axle vehicle. If

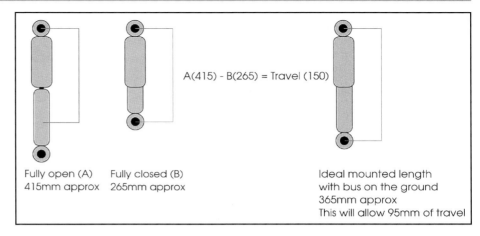

A(415) - B(265) = Travel (150)

Fully open (A) 415mm approx

Fully closed (B) 265mm approx

Ideal mounted length with bus on the ground 365mm approx This will allow 95mm of travel

Diagram 5. Final travel of the shock absorbers should be about 100mm. (Courtesy Creative Engineering)

adjustable spring plates are fitted, there's a final opportunity to adjust the suspension, but the Bus must be back on axle stands to do this. Refer to diagram 4 for the screw settings.

As with any conversion, there

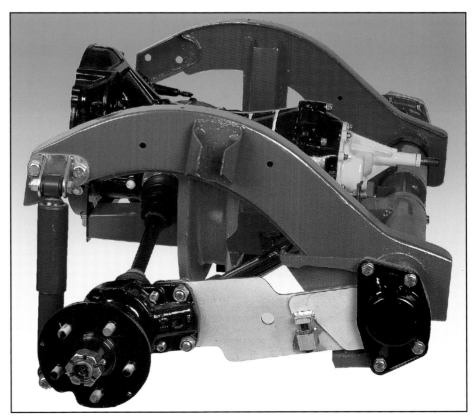

Complete assembly looks like it could have come from the VW factory that way, and gives superb performance. (Courtesy Creative Engineering)

are still jobs left to do, even when the engine is refitted. The brake lines will need to be connected up, and any dubious brake parts changed for new ones, before the whole system is bled and checked for full operation and before driving the Bus on the road. After an initial drive, all the nuts and bolts used in making the conversion should be re-checked as a matter of course. This should be done again after a further 200 miles, and then after 2000 miles purely as a safety precaution.

HEAVY DUTY ANTI-ROLL BARS

Although heavy duty anti-roll bars and camber compensators are aftermarket devices that are best used on Buses not being lowered or modified in any other way, they can help improve the handling on any models. An early Split-screen van uses a swing axle transmission that is very similar to the Beetle. Like the Beetle, it is prone to excessive changes in rear wheel camber, as the suspension moves, which is an inherent factor in this type of suspension design. VW set the rear camber of the Bus in a slightly positive position - that is with the tyres further apart at the top than the bottom - to take account of loads carried in the van. That's fine for general use, but even on sharp corners, the positive camber of the outside rear wheel is increased. This situation forces the wheel to tuck under the van and for the tyre tread to lose contact with the road surface. With the high roll centre of the van, together with the centrifugal force of the cornering manoeuvre, it's all too easy for the back end to suddenly break away-a situation made more dangerous by the rear weight distribution of the Bus.

Before the advent of the VW IRS system, aftermarket manufacturing

Sway-A-Way anti-roll bar is supplied for Beetles, but will fit early swing axle Buses.

companies, such as EMPI, started to develop camber compensator springs to help ease the poor handling situation on the swing axle Beetle and Bus. These kits helped limit the amount of travel by the Bus rear wheels towards positive camber. They were nothing more than a

flat transverse leaf spring that was mounted beneath the transmission and attached to the swing axle shaft tubes.

A similar kit is still available from Sway-A-Way in the US, but has urethane mounts attached to the each end of the bar, where it sits under the axle tubes, and a central metal bracket

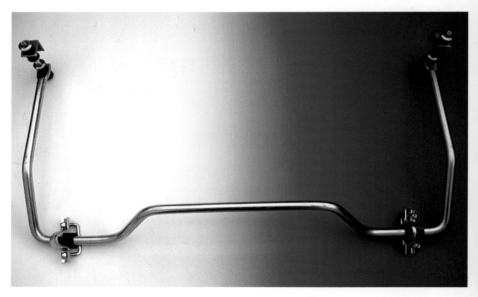

Bay-window Bus owners can fit a heavy duty anti-roll bar kit from Just Kampers or Big Boys Toys.

The mounting for the outer end of the bar uses extensive bushing to provide optimum performance.

with urethane insert to pivot it onto the metal compensator plate that attaches beneath the transmission. This locates onto the studs of the two lowest nuts on either side of the Bus gearbox. It allows the bar to pivot on it, and for the spring effect of the bar to push upwards at the outer ends of the axle shafts to help limit adverse camber changes. It's a 'quick fix' for the early

Bus owners to help improve their vehicle's handling.

For owners of Bay-window Buses, a heavy-duty anti-roll bar kit is available that can aid the handling of an IRS rear suspension. Fitting an anti-roll bar (or anti-sway bar, as it is also known), prevents the body roll that's common on an unmodified Bus, and this should be used in conjunction with a similar bar fitted to the front suspension. These bars are fitted with urethane bushes for longevity and strength. They are available in the US from companies such as Sway-A-Way, or in the UK from Just Kampers or Big Boys Toys.

The kits come with detailed fitting instructions, but in essence the bar mounts transversely across the underside of the Bus beneath the transmission, and is bracketed to the rear chassis frame on either side. At each outer end, the bar is mounted by bushed end-links to a bracket attached to the lower shock absorber mounts. The kit requires four holes drilled in the chassis frame, but is otherwise a bolt-on affair.

OTHER CONVERSION OPTIONS

So far, I've looked at conversions that are possible for most owners to achieve using VW donor parts, or aftermarket performance equipment. Since the essence of this book is to show you what conversions are possible, I am also including outline details of a few 'non-standard' conversions that have been performed (and therefore could be duplicated with specialist help), but will require a considerable amount of work

LATE BUS REAR CHASSIS SECTION CONVERSION

As we've already seen, it is possible to change the entire early Bus front

Australian Bay-window Bus with fitted anti-roll bar, adjustable spring plates, and drop plates. (Courtesy Simon Glen)

suspension for a 1968 - 1969 ball joint style suspension, allowing better brakes to be fitted and enhanced performance. Taking a similar viewpoint, Australian VW Bus specialist Kruzinwagon decided that - rather than convert an early swing axle rear suspension system to IRS - they would fit a complete rear chassis section from a later Bus into an early panel van. Since literally the whole rear part of the chassis was swapped - including the torsion bar housing, control arms, gearbox, hubs, driveshafts etc., and were reused in their original layout (albeit underpinning a different Bus) - the conversion looks like a factory fitting. Add the ball joint front suspension, and the illusion is complete - even down to the matching 5-bolt wheel hubs. However, the problems involved in making this conversion are not to be taken lightly and you would have to refer to the supplier for details on attempting this modification. As it is such a major structural alteration to the Bus we cannot detail it here.

1963 Type 214 Bus fitted with rear chassis section from a 1976 Bus, and a ball joint front suspension. (Courtesy Simon Glen)

specialist parts for future servicing. The removal of the Bus torsion housing effectively leaves a channel into which the complete Beetle torsion bar setup is welded, with only the rear suspension mountings needing to be relocated. Clearance is an issue and, since the Beetle gearbox sits lower in its mounting than the Bus equivalent, the back of the Bus will need raising to achieve a sensible height.

On this conversion, the Beetle rear end was complemented by fitting a complete disc braked and lowered torsion bar Beetle front suspension to the front of the Bus. This conversion required fairly extensive cutting, welding and strengthening to allow the beam to fit, as the mounting plates on the original Bus beam had to be copied and new ones fabricated and welded to the Beetle beam to allow it to bolt straight into the original holes in the chassis rails. The chassis rails were cut to allow unrestricted movement of the track rods, but were

BEETLE IRS REAR CHASSIS SECTION CONVERSION

This is another radical departure from the norm in that the complete Bus swing axle rear suspension and reduction hub gearbox is replaced with a VW Beetle IRS system. Rather than add Beetle parts to the basic structure of the Bus this conversion (carried out by a Bus enthusiast in the UK) completely cuts out the Bus rear torsion bar housing/frame fork and all the running gear from the chassis, and replaces it with the same parts from a late IRS Beetle.

The rationale is that the Beetle IRS conversion is well known for its improved ride and handling, and using this single parts donor for a Bus conversion provides enhanced performance, yet is less expensive than other IRS conversions. It also ensures a greater availability of non-

It may not suit the purists, but this Split-screen Bus has the original torsion bar housing removed, and a complete Beetle IRS rear suspension installed. (Courtesy Richard Parsons)

Beetle IRS suspension in Split-screen Bus. The gearbox sits lower, effectively dropping the rear end. (Courtesy Richard Parsons)

Beetle disc braked and lowered front suspension was also fitted to the front of the Bus. (Courtesy Richard Parsons)

re-strengthened once the final position of the suspension was established.

The installation of Beetle parts into the bus required some ingenuity to mate the Split-window Bus steering box and drag link with Beetle steering components. This was achieved using a combination of Beetle and Bay-window Bus adjustable track rod ends on both near and off sides, and the drag link modified to marry up to the track rod ends. The installation looks neat, and it all works. With braking via a Beetle master cylinder, and coil-over shock absorbers to beef up the suspension, this setup apparently works well on what is purely a road driven Bus that is not destined to carry excessive weight. As a bonus, the Beetle front suspension is slightly narrower than the original. Therefore, although the front is quite low, it has not required any modifications to the front wheelarches like some other Buses. This conversion may not appeal to all, and is definitely not to be considered on Buses where load carrying is still a requirement.

A brace is run between the Beetle chassis forks and the Bus rear chassis member for added strength. (Courtesy Richard Parsons)

RAISING THE BUS
We've looked at a lot of ways of

Porsche Cookie Cutter wheels are fitted with adaptors. The Beetle torsion bar arrangement is clearly visible. (Courtesy Richard Parsons)

are easy enough as most 5-bolt alloys such as the Mercedes 17in, or Audi or Ford wheels bolt up to the 5 x 112mm PCD on these Buses (and the T3 Transporters up to 1992). However for the raised look, particularly on the earlier Split-screen Buses with wide 5 x 205mm PCD wheel bolts, things are a bit trickier, especially since 'tall' tyres will be required. As an example, a standard 14in wheel can be fitted with a high profile tyre such as the Fulda M+S instead of a standard Michelin XZX to achieve a higher ground clearance on the Bus.

Further ground clearance and suspension travel can also be achieved, but this is dependant on the Bus having a 2-litre engine or bigger - anything smaller, like the standard 1600cc engine, and the change to the gearing by fitting taller tyres will be too much. The big wheels and tyres needed to create a Baja Bus will also be much heavier than stock, so allow for this. Using the later suspensions, even in the earlier Bus, will give you a much wider choice of wheels due to the PCD of the later models, so Mercedes wheels

lowering the VW Bus as this is a style, strictly for street use, that is very much favoured in Europe and the US. However, it's not the only way to change the looks (or performance) of your Bus. Different ways of modifying the Bus suspension for off-road use have been developed in Australia where there is a greater culture of using Transporters as 'off-road Kombis' or 'Baja Buses'. These are serious back country vehicles, and a real alternative to a 4WD vehicle in rough, arduous conditions. Such modifications have been performed on T1, T2 and even T3 Transporters. The latter (especially the Synchro four-wheel drive models) are easily raised by fitting heavier coil springs and larger wheels - usually Mercedes 15in, but it is the earlier Split-window and Bay-window modifications we'll be looking at.

When it comes to fitting big wheels to a lowered Bus - particularly a 1971 - 1979 Bay-window - things

View of the modified chassis rails, with Beetle master cylinder fitted. (Courtesy Richard Parsons)

Baja prepared T3 Bus is ready for the outback. (Courtesy Simon Glen)

Both wheels are 14in, but the early 'large' 5-bolt wheel has been fitted with a high profile Fulda M & S tyre to provide additional ground clearance. (Courtesy Simon Glen)

are again the favoured choice. They can be steel 15in x 7in, or alloys in a larger size, providing the tyres you want are available in the correct diameter and width. Something like a BF Goodrich off-road tyre in a 30in x 9.5in x 15in size will just fit under the rear arches, providing the rear spring plates are reset on the torsion bars. Anything larger than this, and the rear wheelarches have to be cut.

Tyre sizes from 31in x 10.5in x 15in right up to 33in x 12.5in x 15in can be accommodated with modification to the rear arches.

There is a seam visible on the inside of the rear wheelarches which, once cut along, will give an arch of approximately the same level as the front. Small rubber wheelarch extensions can then be fitted over the arch to make the modification look like a factory finish. If you are thinking of going taller than a 31in tyre, allow for the effects of full suspension

Heavy-duty coil springs and larger wheels give the T3 transporter off-road capability. (Courtesy Just Kampers)

Bay-window Bus has modified wheelarches to accommodate the larger wheels and tyres necessary for off-road running. (Courtesy Simon Glen)

If your Bus has a sliding door, the larger wheels or wheelarches must not interfere with the door travel, and hinges may need re-working. (Courtesy Simon Glen)

suspension must be considered at the same time as those made to the front suspension, as we've already seen in the last chapter.

For those intent on using their Buses in serious off-road conditions, the shock absorbers will need some thought. There are two common problems associated with shock absorbers used in Transporters off-road. Firstly, the heavy duty Monroe shock absorbers fitted to Australian CKD-assembled (Completely Knocked Down) T2 Transporters in the 1970's can sometimes wear out their rubber bush mounts. This causes not only a constant rattle, but wear on the mounting points. Always fit new units prior to taking a Bus off-road, and consult your dealer to find those that will best suit the length of suspension travel required.

The second shock absorber problem is with the units working loose from their mountings. Front

compression by notching the inner arch to prevent the tyre rubbing on it where it curves downwards at the front and back. Don't forget, that the larger wheels and tyres may not just be a problem for the bodywork surrounding the arch. Remember too that if your Bus has a sliding door it still needs to slide back past the tyre. Any door-to-tyre clearance problems will need to be cured by lengthening the metal arm that levers the door away from the body as it is slid back, and modifying the stop that this arm meets when the door is opened.

Whatever cutting modifications you make to the Bus body, do it with a saw and not a cutting torch for two reasons. Firstly the body metal is relatively thin and will distort with a lot of heat and, secondly, you don't want to risk a torch near the rear mounted fuel tank. Go steady, and cut safely! All the modifications made to the rear

Some Volkswagen owners look down on other Volkswagen owners, especially with a Baja Bus. (Courtesy Simon Glen)

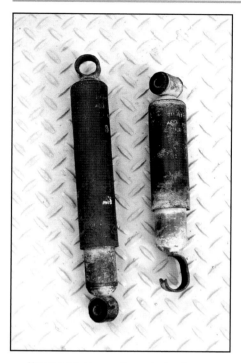

If you plan to go off-road, check your shock absorbers first! Problems like this can happen if the rubber bushes wear out. (Courtesy Simon Glen)

shock absorbers can be made secure by fitting a pair of nuts, tightened up against themselves, to prevent movement of the securing bolt. At the rear, the bottom mounting bolts can be replaced by longer ones with a hole drilled in the end. A pair of nuts are used to secure and lock the mounting bolt, with the added fail-safe of a locking wire to stop the nuts from backing off. This is the most bullet-proof arrangement, and should always be used.

At the top on T1 and T2 Buses, the rear shock absorbers are merely bolted into a captive nut in the vehicle body. The stress of heavy duty use in rough conditions will cause the bolt to flex and ultimately break. Inevitably, a broken piece of bolt will be lodged tight in the captive nut, making it virtually impossible to extract, and leaving you with no shock absorber! Before going off-road, have a 30mm length of channel section steel with a hole in it for the bolt carefully welded

Shock absorber is securely mounted at the bottom with a longer bolt, a pair of locknuts, and a safety wire. (Courtesy Simon Glen)

to the body. This will prevent the bolt flexing and shearing off.

One final point, for Baja Bus owners is that off-roading in rough conditions can work the rear spring plate down below the stop, generally resulting in severe suspension strain or even a broken rear torsion bar. Having a simple metal strap welded across the path of the spring plate will prevent this damage. Naturally, to replace a broken or weak torsion bar would mean the retainer strap would have to be broken away with an angle grinder.

Of course there are more suspension conversions, and new parts and ideas continually become available. In its simplest form, it is possible to raise the rear of your Bus by adjusting the rear spring plates in relation to the torsion bars, whilst at the other extreme, companies such as Custom Bugs & Buses in Australia

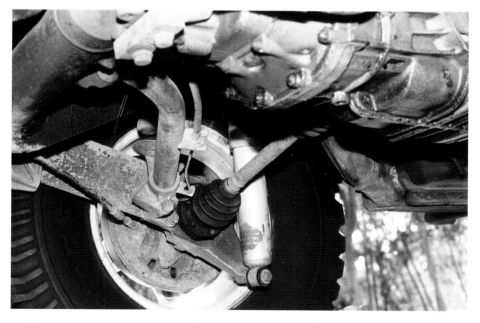

The rear of this Bus has been raised by adjusting the spring plates in relation to the torsion bars. (Courtesy Simon Glen)

To increase this T2 transporter ride height, the suspension, gearbox and engine have all been lowered in relation to the chassis – a major operation. (Courtesy Simon Glen)

have increased the T2 Transporter ride height by lowering the suspension and drive train (complete with engine and gearbox) in the Bus chassis. Such conversions are not straightforward, but show the level of detail that specialists will go to achieve their dream VW Buses.

In the next chapter we look at the chassis, and how to fit an air suspension system for the ultimate Bus performance accessory.

Chapter 4

Chassis & air suspension systems

CHASSIS

The basic structure of the VW Bus chassis - whether beneath the earlier Split-screen model, or the later Bay-window version - is simplicity itself. A strong subframe consisting of longitudinal chassis rails with welded cross members and outer box members (or outriggers) provides a reinforced structure, on which the floor and body panels are attached, to create a unitary construction 'box'.

The design was light years away from other commercial vehicle designs when it was first introduced in 1950, and it has stood the test of time well, with many Transporters still on the road being well over 25 years old. However, good as it is, age and exposure to water and dirt underneath the Bus, will cause the chassis to rot. There comes a time in every Buses' life when the only way to ensure the strength of the chassis is to cut away rusty metal and replace it with new.

Fortunately, all the panels

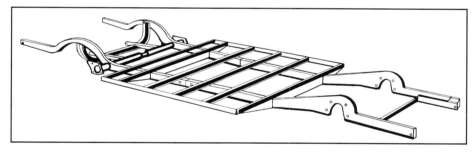

Bus chassis consists of longitudinal chassis rails with welded cross members and outer box members.

Underside of the Bay-window Bus shows the later IRS rear suspension layout.

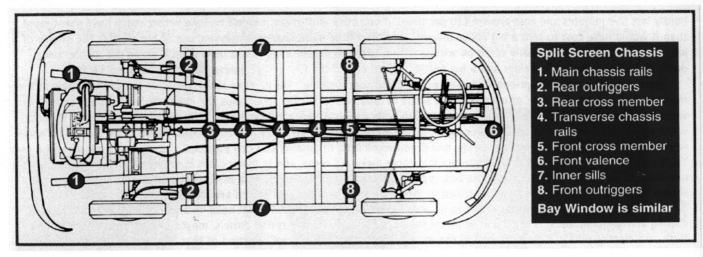

Split Screen Chassis
1. Main chassis rails
2. Rear outriggers
3. Rear cross member
4. Transverse chassis rails
5. Front cross member
6. Front valence
7. Inner sills
8. Front outriggers
Bay Window is similar

Diagramatic view of the Split-screen Bus chassis, complete with engine and running gear.

required for a part, or full, chassis restoration are available from specialist suppliers such as Alan Schofield, VW Heritage Parts, and Just Kampers in the UK, BBT in mainland Europe, Wolfgang International in the US, and Indian Automotive and Vintage Vee-Dub Supplies in Australia.

Since the original chassis is a welded structure, the replacement of

any section means cutting out (with a grinder, or similar) the affected parts, and welding in new sections. As with any welding, always wear proper safety gear such as goggles, and protective gloves to prevent accidents, and if the welding is anywhere near the fuel tank of the Bus, remove it for safety. If you don't have access to welding equipment, or prefer not to tackle

these types of jobs, find a local repair shop or welder who can do this for you.

On the Split screen Bus, all sections of chassis are available as repair panels, including the centre chassis section, cross members, 'T' sections, outer box section, jacking points and the outriggers, amongst others. Similar parts for the Bay-window Bus are also readily available.

Also available are larger under floor plates that link the longitudinal chassis rails, but these were only fitted to German-made T2 Transporters equipped with a factory steel sliding roof or sliding doors both sides, or with the high roof option. These gave added bracing and strength to the vehicle, restricting torsional twisting of the chassis and made them more suitable for rough road conditions. It may seem tempting to fit them to brace the chassis, regardless of the design of the van, but in Europe and North America these give an increased propensity to trap moisture and promote rust - the very thing you are trying to cure!

Apart from the metal parts of the chassis, there are a few other things

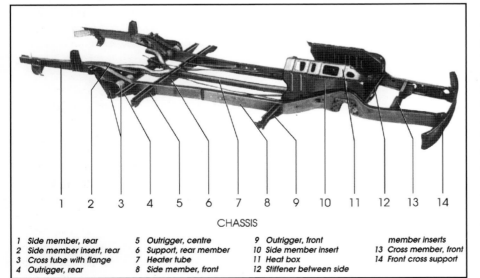

CHASSIS

1 Side member, rear	5 Outrigger, centre	9 Outrigger, front	member inserts
2 Side member insert, rear	6 Support, rear member	10 Side member insert	13 Cross member, front
3 Cross tube with flange	7 Heater tube	11 Heat box	14 Front cross support
4 Outrigger, rear	8 Side member, front	12 Stiffener between side	

Bay-window chassis clearly showing the side member inserts that provide part of the
front seat mountings.

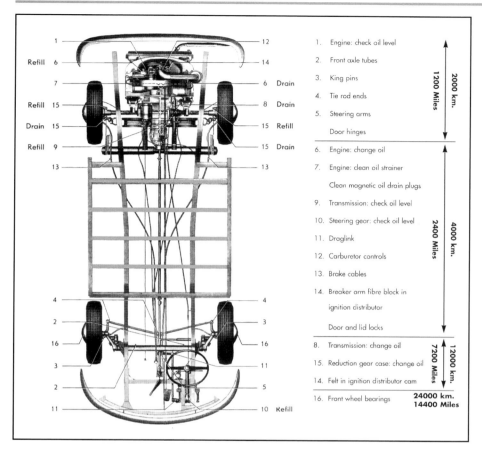

			Interval
1.	Engine: check oil level		
2.	Front axle tubes		
3.	King pins		
4.	Tie rod ends		2000 km. / 1200 Miles
5.	Steering arms		
	Door hinges		
6.	Engine: change oil		
7.	Engine: clean oil strainer		
	Clean magnetic oil drain plugs		
9.	Transmission: check oil level		
10.	Steering gear: check oil level		4000 km. / 2400 Miles
11.	Draglink		
12.	Carburetor controls		
13.	Brake cables		
14.	Breaker arm fibre block in ignition distributor		
	Door and lid locks		
8.	Transmission: change oil		
15.	Reduction gear case: change oil		12000 km. / 7200 Miles
14.	Felt in ignition distributor cam		
16.	Front wheel bearings		24000 km. / 14400 Miles

VW workshop diagram of the Bus running gear lubrication points

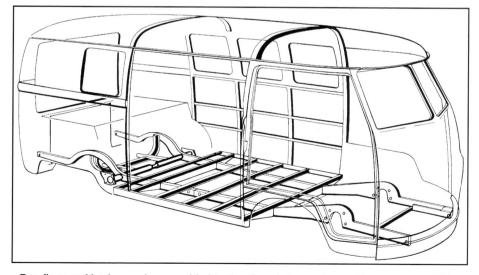

Bus floor and body panels are welded to the chassis to create a unitary structure. This revolutionary design was the basis for VW's legendary 'Box on wheels'.

Bus chassis and body restoration is not to be undertaken lightly! Most chassis members and body panels have now been reproduced, and a complete rebuild is possible. This is a 1959 Bus. (Courtesy Richard Parsons)

that are located on the chassis and can be checked for wear, and replaced, if necessary. If the gear shift rod coupler at the rear of the chassis that attaches to the gearbox 'hockey stick' has not been changed during other modifications, now is the time. They have a tendency to wear, and can give a sloppy shift or even more severe problems with changing gear.

The coupler on the earlier Split-screen Buses is of a different shape to a Type 1 (Beetle) item, so don't be tempted to purchase a performance urethane item for a Type 1, as it won't fit this model. The rubber and metal bonded item from VW (or an aftermarket parts supplier) is still available and plenty strong enough. The Bay-window Buses, however, use the Type 1 style coupler. The two halves of the long gearshift rod that run beneath the van are also supported by a plastic front guide bush, and two similar bushes on the rear section of the rod which should be inspected and replaced if worn. Similarly, two rubber boots sleeve onto the rear section of the rod, and should also be checked.

Beneath the cab floor, where

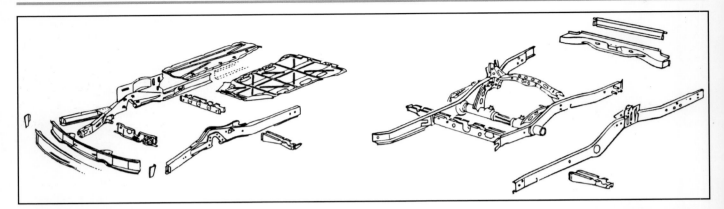

Exploded diagram of the Bay-window Bus chassis parts available for restoration. (Courtesy VW Heritage)

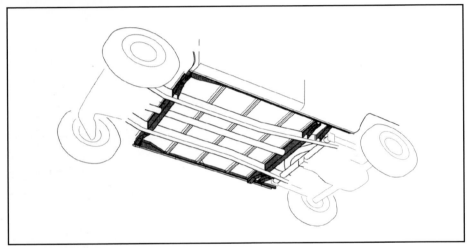

Lower chassis panels available include the sills, outriggers and jacking points. (Courtesy VW Heritage)

the gearshift mounts into the cup at the front of the gearshift rod, a plastic guide bush and metal retaining ring holds the rod into a metal support bracket. The design on chassis prior to number 1074648 did not use the metal retaining ring and were made of a different material. The newer design was introduced to give a more constant and uniform frictional effect, thereby eliminating shift rod noises and sloppiness in the gear change. This sleeve should always be checked and the bush renewed, as wear here can lead to problems with the gear change.

In September 1965 - from chassis number 216028112 - the design of the gearshift lever and support were changed to incorporate a dowel pin at the head of the gearshift rod, running in a forward-mounted bush. On these models, this bush should also be inspected and replaced if wear is apparent.

GEARSHIFTERS & QUICKSHIFT KITS

For performance use, the stock Bus gearshifter doesn't provide the best characteristics to enhance any other modifications made to the vehicle, particularly in terms of the engine and transmission. It has a long 'throw' to

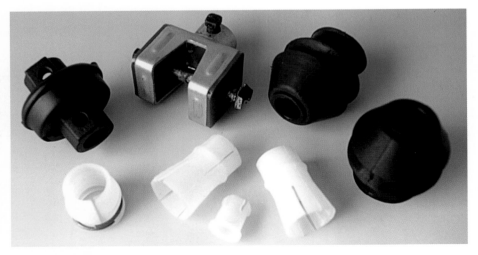

(Back L-R) Split-screen Bus gear coupler; urethane Bay-window coupler, gear rod rubber boots. (Front L-R) gearshift guide bush; plastic guide bushes.

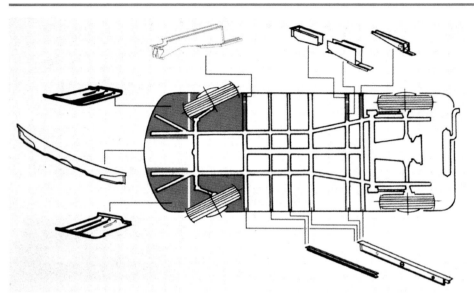

**Two views of the large underfloor plates fitted to German Buses requiring extra torsional strength. You don't have to turn your Bus over to see them!
(Courtesy Simon Glen)**

**Underside body and chassis parts for the Bay-window Bus available from Just Kampers.
(Courtesy Just Kampers)**

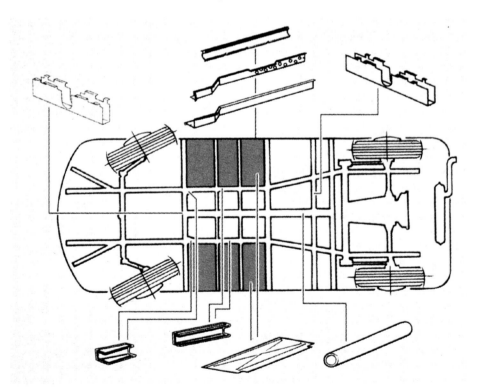

been quick to see the possibilities of improving the basic design, and there is now a wide range of performance shifters to choose from. Manufactured by US companies such as Scat, EMPI and Gene Berg, the essence of all the designs is twofold. One, to provide smoother gear selection whilst reducing the throw of the lever, and two, to improve the ease of reverse gear selection. The styles differ considerably, and there is no substitute for trying each of the designs (either on a company demonstrator vehicle, or a friend's vehicle) to see which suits you and your Bus best.

The 'Hurst' style shifter - now made by EMPI - uses a 'trigger' style sliding section to the outside of the shaft which, when lifted, engages reverse as the lever is pulled backwards. A Scat manufactured

the lever, and an unusual arrangement for engaging reverse gear. You have to press down on the lever and slide it over towards the left side of the vehicle before pulling it backwards.

Aftermarket suppliers have

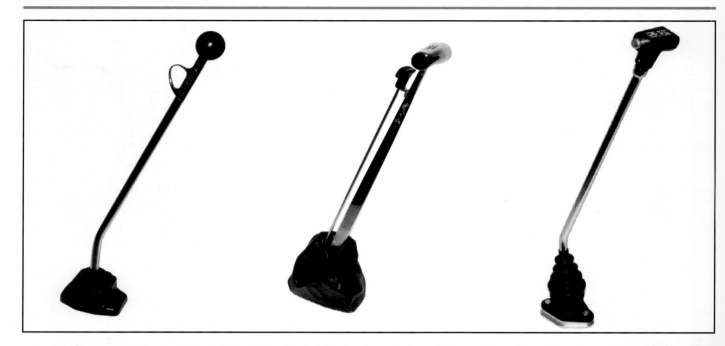

Hurst-style trigger shifter is on the left, Scat Drag-Fast shifter is shown in the middle, and Gene Berg short-throw shifter with reverse button is on the right. (Courtesy Custom & Speed Parts)

dual-handle version is also available with 'T'-handled top, called the 'Drag-Fast' shifter. The design incorporates a separate lever at the front with a smaller handle to pull it upwards to engage reverse.

Shifters, such as those made by Gene Berg and other suppliers, have a short-throw lever and use a push button set into one side of the handle. When the button is engaged and the lever is pulled back, reverse is selected.

The Berg item is also available in a locking design which provides not only a superior gear change, but also added security. This item uses what is termed a 'Quickshift' baseplate as its mounting.

QUICKSHIFT KIT

The Quickshift kit is designed to reduce the stock gear lever movement by 40%, and makes gear changing less of a chore. The kit is available from a

number of suppliers such as Bluebird customs in the UK, and comes in several parts consisting of a baseplate for the gear lever housing, a rounded block that fits over the lever itself, and two long threaded bolts. Bluebird also supply a complete kit comprising a chromed gear lever, and top extension for those requiring a custom look.

Fitting the Quickshift kit is very straightforward, and consists of firstly unscrewing the gear lever knob, then removing the rubber gaiter that fits around the base of the lever (which can be replaced upon reassembly if it is split). With a 13mm spanner, undo the two bolts that hold the lever baseplate down into the recess in the cab floor. The spring underneath it will push the plate up, so work from side to side to avoid straining the components unnecessarily.

Lift the lever away from the floor, but leave the separate, greased, plate - which incorporates the reverse

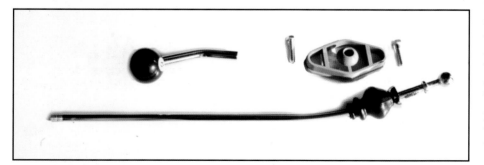

Bluebird Customs Quickshift kit and chromed gear lever with extension, and 'pool ball' top.

Max Hydraulics air suspension kit gives lowered stance, full adjustability, and a comfortable ride. (Courtesy Jon Betts)

Large air bags are made of a spring constructed rubber in the shape of bellows, and are fitted to special brackets. This is a Max Hydraulics kit. (Courtesy John Clewer)

gear lockout guide - in place. Put the Quickshift baseplate directly over this, and try not to lose the position of the reverse plate, as it can be adjusted by moving it around slightly.

Next, slip the lever out of the metal baseplate, and fit the rounded block, that came in the kit, over the top of the existing one. Grease this well and then refit the baseplate over this. Now simply fit the lever/baseplate over the Quickshift base, and use the longer bolts with the original washers to hold it all in place. Adjust the mechanism before finally tightening it down. The result will give a noticeable reduction in gear lever movement when engaging the gears.

AIR SUSPENSION KITS
Max Hydraulics' air suspension kit
A need for more refined suspension kits for the VW Bus has led to a number of exciting new products, including lowering/raising kits, being developed and becoming generally available on the market. Principal amongst these has been the availability of air suspension kits, which have largely overtaken the earlier hydraulic kits that were developed for vehicles in the 1980s.

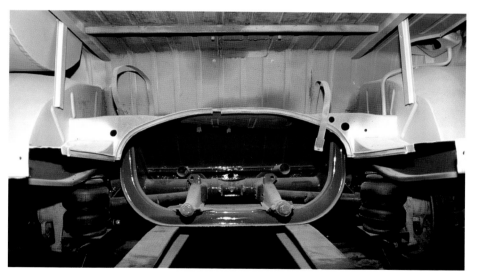

Rear engine bay of a 1962 Split-screen Bus shows the hydraulic system fitted, awaiting installation of IRS gearbox and high performance engine. (Courtesy John Clewer)

Bellows can be a tapered sleeve design for fitting in restricted space.
(Courtesy Jon Betts)

Reservoir tank is used to provide instant height adjustment to the bags, with the compressor refilling the tank when the pressure drops below a certain level.
(Courtesy Jon Betts)

Electrically-driven air compressor takes only about 10 seconds to achieve full lift, and can be concealed in a cupboard.
(Courtesy Jon Betts)

These have given Buses an increasingly comfortable ride, even at extremes of suspension lowering, as well as allowing ride height to be adjusted. This facility enables the Bus to be driven safely over uneven road surfaces at a normal height, but dropped down quickly for aesthetic looks at any time.

One of the best-known companies supplying air suspension kits in the UK is Max Hydraulics, with its 'Maxaire' system. The company still supplies full hydraulic systems, but it is the air system we'll look at here.

Since the kits use non-VW parts and engineering, let's just review the basic parts of the system to understand what happens when using one of these kits. At the front and back of the Bus, large air bags are fitted which can be inflated or deflated to make the vehicle rise or fall by around 5in - 6in when required. These bags - which are basically the same design as those fitted to HGV trucks, and luxury motor vehicles like Rolls Royce - are made of a spring constructed rubber and high strength fabric in the shape of bellows, or a tapered sleeve where there are space restrictions.

The bags supplied in the Maxaire system are manufactured by Firestone (one of the world's largest producer of air bags), and are available in many sizes and capacity ratings. The bags mount to specially fabricated metal brackets front and back (which are both bolted and welded on), and allow the Bus to sit very low when they are fully deflated but, once pumped up, they will raise the Bus to a near-stock height.

The bags can be pumped up with

Four control switches, one for each corner of the Bus, are situated under the dash within driver reach. A pressure gauge is also included.
(Courtesy Jon Betts)

an ordinary tyre pump if an inflation point is rigged into the system, but this rather defeats the benefit of quick adjustment. To raise the vehicle up by inflating the bags with an electrically driven air compressor (pump) takes only about 10 seconds to achieve full lift, so this is certainly the best option. It is even possible to achieve quicker lifts (in a fashion similar to hydraulics)

Front air bag fitted to specially constructed bracket. These will each lift up to 2500lb.
(Courtesy Jon Betts)

by using multi-pump and tank setups and large-bore pipework, but this is costly and a luxury that most people may have to do without. To pump the bags up, the air compressor is used in conjunction with a reservoir tank.

Originally, Max Hydraulics used UK-sourced pumps and valves, with in-house built cylinders, but they have now changed to custom units from the US, as these are better suited to lowriders. Various types have been used, including CCE Hydraulic Products and Easy Street Air Products items, though currently the pumps are Firestone units producing a maximum of 150psi at 12 volts. These will happily run from the standard Bus 12-volt battery, with no need for additional batteries, unlike an hydraulic system.

The air is supplied to the bags from the reservoir tank, which in turn is filled by the compressor when the pressure drops below a set level. By having a reservoir of air available, the suspension can be instantly adjusted. One of the beauties of this system is that the air tank (3 gallon or larger) and the compressor are relatively small, and can be 'hidden' in a cupboard on the Bus. This is really the biggest advantage over hydraulics which use much larger pumps, coupled with multiple batteries, making them much harder to position successfully without taking up too much internal space within the Bus.

The air lines that carry the pressurised air are capable of withstanding 180psi, and are 6mm nylon tubes, which is more than adequate. Connections are made with simple push-fit connectors. In the unlikely event that a line split, and system pressure was lost, the Bus would simply ride on the suspension bump stops - a necessary reason for retaining the original VW suspension

Space is limited at the rear of this Bus, so a pair of tapered sleeve air bags are used. These will hold up to 2100lb, and will give progressive springing.
(Courtesy Jon Betts)

bump stops. They will also prevent the metal air bag end caps hitting together. A line failure can be fixed using a standard in-line connector without the need for special tools, so it's always worth carrying one with you, just in case!

The last part of the system are the switches, valves and gauges. The easiest way to control the flow of air is with electric switchgear (rather than manual), mounted on the dashboard (or in a special panel), somewhere near the driver. These control the electric solenoid valves that are used to regulate the airflow from the tank to the bags. It is common to mount four switches - one for each corner of the Bus - to allow different combinations of lift, depending how they are wired up. You may want a straightforward up and down at the front and back, or a side to side arrangement if you are trying to replicate a hydraulic-type system. Whichever combination you

Creative Engineering uses precision machined rods through the upper and lower torsion tubes, with the air bags mounted on special brackets.

changing the carrying requirements of your van to allow for extra weight or to tow a trailer, for example, it is better to install the larger bags and simply increase the pressure in them to compensate as and when required. Doing this will not affect the ride of the Bus.

Fitting a Maxaire system - like any other modification to the suspension on a Bus - can affect the alignment of the front wheels. The manufacturers have found, however, that by setting the front wheel alignment with the ride height set somewhere in the middle of the furthest points of adjustment, the setting can be used as a 'normal' cruising height, and that the front end geometry will be correct. Moving the adjustment up or down from here, for short periods, to create a raised or lowered look will not cause particular problems as long as the setting is returned to normal afterwards.

In fact the quality of ride of this system will be as good as - if not better than - a standard unaltered suspension system. If you are planning on

seriously lowering your Bus, then this is a system that must be considered for the ultimate ride at both the front and back of the vehicle. It is not a cheap proposition but, if fitted correctly and well-maintained, it will last indefinitely.

Creative Engineering's air suspension kit

Working on a similar principle to the Max Hydraulics system, the new air suspension kit for 1955 - 1967 Split-screen Buses from Creative Engineering allows an Independent Front Suspension (IFS) and an Independent Rear Suspension (IRS). The kit is still in the final stages of development, at the time of writing, but will be available soon. Similar kits will available for the later Bay-window Buses, and Beetles too.

The basic kit works with the same engineering at the back as the Maxaire kit, but it's at the front that a major difference is instantly noticeable. Rather than stay with the VW-designed torsion bar front suspension system, lifted and lowered by air bags, the

use, remember to fit monitoring gauges to the dashboard to keep an eye on the air pressure in the bags.

Mounting the brackets for the system does require some welding, so be prepared to enlist the skills of a competent welder if you don't feel capable of attempting this part yourself. The brackets are mounted under the cab floor at the front, and near the rear shock absorbers at the rear - though this depends on which system you use (bellows or sleeve type). Location of the brackets is very important as the bags must be protected from any moving suspension parts or wheels/ tyres to prevent the risk of them being damaged and failing in operation.

The bellows-style air bags will each lift up to 2500lb, whilst the sleeve type will lift 2100lb each. This provides progressive springing due to the 'corrugated' design of their sidewalls. If you are considering dramatically

**Creative Engineering kit uses 'Weedeater' air suspension. The 4000 kit has a short lift time of just 5-6 seconds on both front/back and side/side control.
(Courtesy Creative Engineering)**

How low can your Bus go? Just press the button and lower away. (Courtesy Jon Betts)

equipment, and the engineering of the IFS, results in an air suspension package that eliminates the main problems of suspension lowering, namely a harsh ride, and difficulties in making quick adjustments. It isn't a cheap kit, but it is a serious investment for someone planning on keeping and using their Bus for many years.

CONCLUSION

As with any section of the performance market, there will always be new products and new ideas entering the field. The market for Bus parts has grown dramatically over the last few years, and there are no signs of it abating. All of this is good news for the Bus lover who wishes to improve the suspension, braking or handling of his or her Bus. As new products appear, they are often reviewed in the specialist VW press, and you will have to decide for yourself whether they offer you the type of features that will benefit your vehicle, and are within your price range.

It's always advisable to obtain as much information on specialist parts, and their fitting, from the manufacturers or retailer before you part with your cash. Ask yourself "Will they be easy to fit? Will they do what you are expecting them to do when they are fitted? Will they require specialist tools or knowledge to fit?". If possible, talk to other owners/drivers who have used them, and can recommend them.

There are also a growing number of specialist VW clubs catering for the needs of those with both Split-screen and Bay-window Buses. Making a small investment to join their ranks may well pay dividends when you need to talk to other like-minded enthusiasts. Above all, enjoy driving your Bus and have fun!

torsion bars are dispensed with altogether, and precision machined rods are fitted through the torsion tubes top and bottom. The ends of each rod are located with specially made bearings and bushes, and the bottom bar has a rose joint fitted to its outer end, which also attaches to the bracket mounting the air bag. Since the weight of the front of the vehicle is now effectively riding on the joint, this is a load rated part.

Specially fabricated brackets, that act as supports for the large bellows-style air bags at each side of the suspension, run parallel to the ground, and attached to the bottom shock absorber mounts. The air bags used in this system are the same design as those fitted to Rolls Royce cars. The design of the bracket on which they mount allows them to rise and fall in a plane parallel to the ground for ultimate smoothness. It also allows them to act as bump stops in

the system. Top plates also locate the upper part of the air bags to the VW suspension.

The pump, solenoids, tank, gauges and all wiring and hoses are supplied by Air Ride Technologies in the US - a foremost name in air suspension systems. These come in various stages of kit. The 'Weedeater 2000' kit has the pump, control panel, wiring loom, solenoids , 2-gallon tank, airlines and all fittings, and offers a front/back control, and lift-time of 8-10 seconds. The larger 'Weedeater 4000' kit has a shorter lift time (5-6 seconds), and front/back and side/side control. The top-of-the-range 'Weedeater 4600' kit has two separate compressors and two 3-gallon tanks, and can offer very fast front/back and side/side control. Lifting can be accomplished in a mere 2 seconds with this extremely powerful air suspension kit.

The high quality of the pumping

Appendix 1

Suppliers & clubs

UK AND EU SUPPLIERS

Alan H Schofield
Vale House
Dinting Lane
Glossop
Derbyshire
SK13 7GA
UK
Tel: +0044 (0)1457 854267
www.ahschofield.co.uk

Specialist manufacturer of quality repair panels and parts, no longer produced for Bay-window and Split-screen Buses.

BBT
Nijverheidsstraat 4
2960 St. Job in t'Goor
Belgium
Tel: +0032 (0)3 633 2222
www.BBT4VW.com

Specialist VW parts supplier for NOS, reproduction and aftermarket parts.

Beetles (UK) Ltd
The Stables
Tanhouse Lane
Rangeworthy
South Gloucestershire
BS37 7LP
UK
Tel: +0044 (0)1454 228999
www.beetles-uk.com

Brand new VW T2 vans and campers; new and used parts.

Big Boys Toys
13 Breach Road
West Thurrock
Essex
RM20 3NR
UK
Tel: +0044 (0)1708 861827
www.bigboyztoys.co.uk

Bus Boys boomerang rear adjuster plates '68-'79; Bus Boys straight axle and IRS kit; Albatross front lowering adjusters; EMPI front and rear heavy duty anti-roll bars; Spax and KYB shock absorbers; brake and suspension parts.

Bluebird Customs
32 Whalley Road
Gt.Harwood
Lancs
BB6 7TF
UK
Tel: +0044 (0)1254 888416
www.bluebird-type2.co.uk

Foksy adjuster; urethane spring plate grommets; stainless steel braided brake hose kits; steering column bushes for T1 and T2; gear lever kit and gear lever extensions.

BPS Campers
Portsmouth Road
Bramshott Chase
Hindhead
Surrey
GU26 6DE
UK

Tel: +0044 (0)1428 608100
www.bpscampers.co.uk

VW camper restoration and T2 accessories

Car Parts Direct
160 Burton Road
Derby
DE1 1TN
UK
Tel: +0044 (0)1332 290833
www.carparts-direct.co.uk

Rossini cross drilled and grooved performance brake discs for Buses

Classic-Leisure and Commercial
Unit 23
Britannia Trading Estate
Britannia Road
Milnsbridge
Huddersfield
HD3 4QG
UK
Tel: +0044 (0)1484 462393

Easi-Lo IRS Bus brackets (require shaping to fit torsion tubes).

Creative Engineering
Enford Mead
Gains Cross
Durweston
Blandford
Dorset
DT11 0QW
UK
Tel: +0044 (0)1258 863600
www.creative-engineering.com

IRS conversion kit; lowered and adjustable spring plates; IRS chassis legs; billet wheel adaptors; CSP disc brake conversion; CSP 205mm PCD/ Creative custom PCD disc conversion; air ride suspension kits for Split-screen Bus front and rear.

Custom and Speed Parts Autoteile
GmbH (CSP)
Am Redder 3
22941 Bargteheide
Germany
Tel: +0049 4532 202622/ +49 4532 23240
www.customspeedparts.com

CSP disc brake conversion kits, including vented discs with 4-piston calipers. Full range of restoration and performance parts.

Harry Harpic's
Brookside Works
4 Springfield Drive
Westcliff-on-Sea
Essex
UK
Tel: +0044 (0)1702 391756

Lowering T2s, IRS conversions and ball joint front suspension conversions for Split-screen Buses; front suspension lowering kits; dual circuit master cylinder and servo assisted brake system conversions for Split-screen Buses; narrowed front beams; wheel adaptors.

Just Kampers
Unit 1
Stapely Manor
Long Lane
Odiham
Hants
RG29 1JE
UK
Tel: +0044 (0)845 1204720
www.justkampers.co.uk

Parts and accessories for 1968 - 1992 VW campers and transporters; front suspension lowering kits; sway bars and performance shock absorbers.

Machine 7 Automotive
Unit 40
Caldecote Drive
Caldecot
Nuneaton
Warwickshire
CV10 0TW
UK
Tel: +0044 (0)7002 622446
www.machine7.co.uk

Wheel adaptors for Bay-window bus/T25 to early VW 205mm five-bolt wheel pattern, Porsche 130mm five-bolt pattern, or any other five-bolt pattern.

Max Hydraulics
Tel: +0044 (0)1886 833253
www.maxhydraulics.co.uk

Hydraulic suspension and air-ride suspension systems for Buses.

Red 9 Design
10 Jasmine Walk
Evesham
Worcestershire
WR11 6AL
UK
Tel: +0044 (0)1386 421179
www.red9design.co.uk

Straight and lowered spring plates; EZ rider front end lowering kit; adjustable dampers, suspension bushes.

The Bus Station
23 Exmouth Road
Southsea
Hampshire
PO5 2QL
UK
Tel: +0044 (0)23 9234 5000
www.thebusstation.co.uk

Suppliers of Bus parts, including ready-to-fit copper brake pipe kits and connectors for '68-69, '70 only, and '71-79 Buses, and VW paints.

The Split Van Centre
169, Stafford Road
Wallington
Surrey
SM6 9BT
UK
Tel: +0044 (0)20 8286 8484
www.splitvan.co.uk

Parts and accessories for split-screen vans.

Volksheaven
Tel: +0044 (0)1302 351355
www.volksheaven.co.uk

IRS conversion kit

VW Heritage Parts Centre Ltd
Hollands Lane
Henfield
West Sussex
BN5 9QY
UK
Tel: +0044 (0)1273 495800
www.vwheritage.com

Genuine VW repair and restoration parts

US SUPPLIERS

Air Ride Technologies Inc
350 South St. Charles Street
Jasper
Indiana 47546
USA
Tel: +001 812 482 2932
www.ridetech.com

Air ride suspension systems

Bus Boys Inc
18595 East Lake Blvd
Redding
CA 96003
USA

Tel: +001 530 244 1616

Albatross front lowering adjusters; IRS and straight axle conversion kits; boomerang rear adjuster plates '68-'79.

CSP USA
140 E. Santa Clara St
#15, Arcadia
CA 91006
USA
Tel: +001 626 445 0108
www.customspeedparts.com

CSP disc brake conversions

Old Speed Air-Cooled Specialists
7311 Madison Street
Unit A
Paramount
CA 90723
USA
Tel: +001 310 531 4190

IRS Bus brackets (pre-shaped to torsion bar tubes); IRS kits; disc brake conversions.

Rocky Mountain Motorworks
1003 Tamarac Parkway
Woodland Park
CO 80863
USA
Tel: +001 800 258 1996
www.motorworks.com

CSP disc brake conversions

Wolfgang International
1117 Parkview Ave
Redding
CA 96001
USA
Tel: +001 530 246- 4264
www.wolfgangint.com

Early Bus IRS conversion kit; rebuilt kingpin spindles; lowered kingpin spindles; straight swing-axle conversion kit (lowers rear); '68-79 sway-bar kit; wheel adaptors; master cylinder adaptor kit for Bus disc brakes; front disc brake conversion kit; rebuilt Bus steering boxes; reconditioned steering arms and new ball joints.

AUSTRALIAN SUPPLIERS

Custom Bugs and Buses
6/14 Peach Tree Street
Penrith
Sydney
2750
Australia
Tel: +0061 (0)2 4722 9313

Specialists in Bus suspension and brake modifications; disc brake kits; adjustable spring plates.

Harding European
22b Reginald Street
Rocklea
Brisbane
Qld 4106
Australia
Tel: +0061 (0)7 3276 7477
www.hardingeuropean.com.au

New and used performance and restoration parts

Indian Automotive
10 Copeland Street
Kingswood
Sydney
Australia
Tel: +0061 (0)2 4731 6444
www.kruizinwagon.com.au

Custom and reproduction T2 products; T2 King Pin spindles rebuilt, stock or dropped; adjustable front beams; adjustable spring plates; Beach Kit high lift suspension kit for '71-'79 T2; T1 and T2 vehicle modifications; Kruizinwagon IRS kit.

Mick Motors
96 Toombul Road
Northgate 4013
Brisbane
Australia
Tel: +0061 (0)7 3266 8133
www.mickmotors.com.au

VW spare parts and service

Muller & Muller Pty.Ltd
999 Canterbury Road
Lakemba
NSW 2195
Sydney
Australia
Tel: +0061 (0)2 9759
1818/0504/2078

T3 specialists, and VW spare parts.

Sherman Conversions
17 Ashton Street
Labrador
Gold Coast 4215
Australia
Tel: +0061 (0)7 5537 7770

Manufacturers and designers of VW
performance parts; 4-wheel disc-brake
systems; suspension modifications.

Vintage Vee-Dub Supplies
Unit 1
11B Harp Street
Campsie 2194
Sydney
Australia
Tel: +0061 (0)2 9789 1777

Body panels; suspension repair
and improvement parts; gas shock
absorbers.

Volks Engineering
10 McGrath Street
Waterford
Brisbane 4133
Australia
Tel: +0061 (0)7 3200 5212

Specialists in raising Buses, and
modifications for off-road.

Volks-Mod
20 George Street
Southport
Gold Coast 4215
Australia
Tel: +0061 (0)755 329388

Specialists in raising T1, T2 and T3
Transporters.

Web site for Baja Bus owners: www.
baja.com/kombi.

CLUBS (UK)
The Split-Screen Van Club
21 Nabwood Road
Shipley
W.Yorks
BD1P 4AG
UK
Tel: +0044 (0)1274 596 564
www.ssvc.org.uk

VW Type 2 Owners Club
57 Humphrey Avenue
Bromsgrove
Worcestershire
B60 3JD
UK
Tel: +0044 (0)1527 872194
www.vwt2oc.org.uk

Vanfest website:
www.vanfest.org

CLUBS (US)
SOTO (Society of Transporter
Owners)
275 Fairchild
108A, Chico
CA 95973
USA
www.soto.org

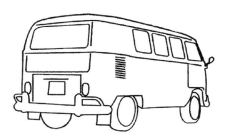

Appendix 2

Chassis numbers & model designations

USE OF TERM IRS (INDEPENDENT REAR SUSPENSION)

The term 'IRS' is used throughout the book to indicate those models (the T2 'bay-window' and T3 Type 24 and Type 25 'wedge') fitted with the two CV-jointed driveshafts, and diagonal control arms, on each side of the gearbox. As explained in the main text, the term 'IRS' is a misnomer. All the pre-1967 Buses are, strictly speaking, fitted with independent rear suspensions, even the swing-axle (Split-screen) models. However, the term has become the accepted description of the later type of rear suspension, and is thus used here also.

VW BUS CHASSIS NUMBERS 1950 - 1979

Whilst the VW Bus did not use a true, separate, chassis in the accepted engineering sense - its torsional strength relied upon the body being welded into a unitized structure

US market VIN plate in windscreen.

supported by this reinforcement frame - the term will be used here, and throughout the book, as this is its popular description.

Identifying and dating a VW Bus is very straightforward, once the

system of numbering that appears on the VIN plate (Vehicle Identity Plate) is understood. This VIN plate contains more information than a chassis number alone, and it is essential to refer to this when ordering parts.

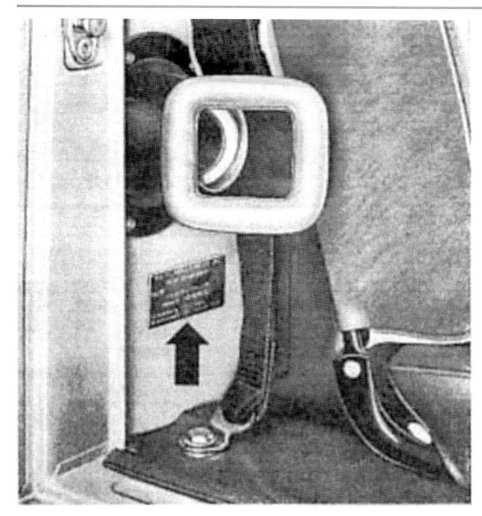

Bay-window VIN plate is usually on bulkhead behind front seats.

VIN plate for 1987 T3 VW Caravelle built to British specifications. (Courtesy Simon Glen)

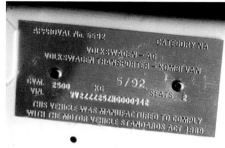

VIN or 'compliance plate' for 1992, for vehicles destined for Australia. (Courtesy Simon Glen)

From 01 Jan 1969, all US vehicles - whether VW or not - have a small, additional, VIN plate which only has the vehicle identification number (i.e.: chassis number) on it, and is attached to the top of the left side of the dashboard near the windscreen so it is visible from outside the vehicle. This is sometimes referred to as the 'chassis plate', and is not to be confused with the rectangular Vehicle Identity Plate found on all Transporters made in Germany. This indicates weight limits, the options fitted to the vehicle and, in some countries, the actual date of manufacture.

This plate is located in the engine compartment (on the vertical surface to the right of the engine) on all Split-screen (T1), vehicles built before late 1963, and thereafter inside the cab on the driver's side of the overhead fresh air duct. On Bay-windows (T2), the Vehicle Identity Plate is found either on the heater ducting under the dashboard in front of the driver or on the bulkhead behind the driver's seat. On T3s it is found on the heater ducting in front of the driver.

The number is also embossed into the sheet metal of the vehicle, since both Vehicle Identity Plates and VIN plates are merely riveted into place and could otherwise be drilled out and removed. In most countries the only legal vehicle identification is the actual chassis number or VIN stamped onto a metal part of the body.

On Split-screen vans (T1s) and early Bay-windows (T2s), this is stamped into the sheet metal on the right of the engine, close to the battery. On 1972 and later T2s, it is stamped on a raised panel just inside the engine bay, on the left side, at the very back of the vehicle. On T3s, it is

(Left) 1972 – 1979 T2 Transporter chassis number on raised panel in engine bay. (Right) Non-German chassis number. The upper plate gives factory information – in this case in Australia. (Courtesy Simon Glen)

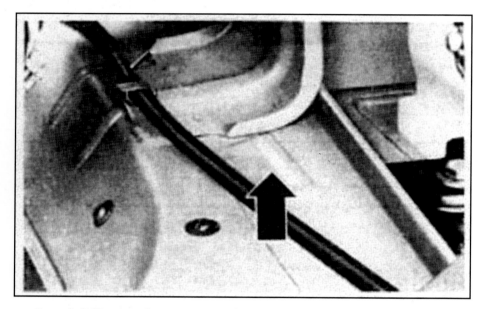

On early Split-screen Buses and early Bay-window Buses, chassis number is also stamped into the bodywork in the engine bay.

stamped on the rear facing part of the cross-member chassis rail just behind the right front wheel arch. It can only be seen by lying on the ground just behind the right front wheel.

Chassis numbers prior to 1956 are prefixed '20', but this was then dropped. The remaining six figures continued in the same sequence until the end of the 1964 model year (July 1964). From the start of the 1965 model year (August 1964) a new system was introduced using the first two digits to denote the model type of the vehicle, and the third digit, the year of manufacture. The model types - or 'designations' as VW referred to them - are listed in the separate section following the chassis numbering.

After the three-digit prefix, a new six-digit numbering sequence ran from the beginning of each new model year, starting from 000 001. From 1970, the fourth digit is always a '2' - which stands for the second generation of Transporters (T2).

The actual chassis number or VIN stamped on the bodywork of all Transporters has a little star stamped at the beginning and end of the chassis number, thus: *226 2 123 456*. In some cases, the little star at the beginning and end of a chassis number is replaced by a tiny 'VW' logo.

This numbering coincided with the return to work in August after the factory's summer break. It became the time when most major changes to the vehicle design were introduced. This aided production efficiency, as changes could be made to a vehicle at one time, and gave the vehicles' marketing an additional boost, as the 'new model' provided enhanced sales opportunities. However, some smaller changes were made by VW between these times, so always quote the exact chassis number - not just the first three digits - when ordering parts.

VW BUS CHASSIS NUMBERS 1950 - 1979

The * at the beginning and end of each number is not shown in the following list, to aid clarity, but will be seen on the number stamped into the VW bodywork.

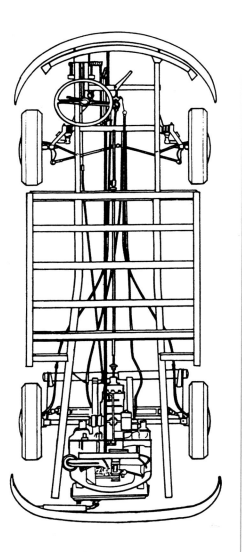

Split-screen Bus/T1 (1950 -1967)

This listing is taken from the official VW publication 'Progressive Refinements'.

1950 (March - Dec)	20-000 001 to 20-008 112
1951 (dates now shown Jan - Dec)	20-008 113 to 20-020 112
1952	20-020 113 to 20-041 857
1953	20-041 858 to 20-070 431
1954	20-070 432 to 20-110 603
1955	20-110 604 to 20-160 735
1956	160 736 to 223 216
1957	223 217 to 315 209
1958	315 210 to 416 082
1959	416 083 to 546 843
1960	546 844 to 710 609
1961	710 610 to 882 314
1962	882 315 to 989 985 (-August)
'New 1963 Model Year' (Sep-)	989 986 to 1 047 967
1963 (Jan-Dec)	1 047 968 to 1 222 500
1964 (Jan-July)	1 222 501 to 1 328 871

1965 (From August 1964, dates were shown as model year, running from 1 August - 31 July. The actual chassis number now being prefixed with three digits to show model type and year. i.e.: '21' is a panel van, '5' the year of 1965, and the remaining six-digit number is the sequential production figure

	215 000 001 to 215 176 339
1966	216 000 001 to 216 179 668
1967	217 000 001 to 217 148 459

Bay-window Bus/T2 (1968 - 1979)

1968	218 000 001 to 218 202 251
1969	219 000 001 to 219 238 131
1970	210 2 000 001 to 210 2 248 837
1971	211 2 000 001 to 211 2 276 560
1972	212 2 000 001 to 212 2 246 946
1973	213 2 000 001 to 213 2 254 657
1974	214 2 000 001 to 214 2 194 943
1975	215 2 000 001 to 215 2 155 145
1976	216 2 000 001 to 216 2 186 542
1977	217 2 000 001 to 217 2 165 421
1978	218 2 000 001 to 218 2 161 568
1979	219 2 000 001 to 219 2 153 964

The chassis numbers of Bay-window models on the previous page refers to those manufactured or assembled in Germany, Ireland, South Africa, Indonesia and Australia. The design did continue in production in Mexico until 1997 and is still in production in Brazil. Since 1997, these 'new' T2 Bay-window models - imported from Brazil - have been marketed in Britain by Beetles (UK).

The Brazilian Bay-window chassis numbers are therefore listed below:

1998 models (from 1 August 1997)	WP 000 001
1999 models (from 1 August 1998)	XP 000 001
2000 models (from 1 August 1999)	YP 000 001
2001 models (from 1 August 2000)	1P 000 001
2002 models (from 1 August 2001)	2P 000 001
2003 models (from 1 August 2002)	3P 000 001

MODEL DESIGNATIONS
Split-screen Bus/T1 (1950-1967)

21 - Panel van with loading doors - (Kastenwagen)
22 - Microbus (9-seater) - (Kleinbus)
23 - Kombi (window van, with seating) with loading doors
24 - Microbus (8-seater) de luxe (Samba)
25 - Microbus (7-seater) de luxe (Samba) walk-through. LHD only
26 - Single or double cab pick-up - (Pritschenwagen)
27 - Ambulance - (Krankenwagen)
28 - Microbus (7-seater) walk-through. LHD only.

Bay-window Bus/T2 (1968-1979)

21 - Panel van with sliding doors
22 - Microbus (7, 8 and 9 seats)
23 - Kombi (window van) with sliding doors
24 - Microbus (8 and 9 seats) with sunroof
26 - Single or double cab pick-up
27 - Ambulance
28 - Microbus (7 seater) walk-through.

Third generation 'Wedge' Bus/T3 (August 1979-date)

Note: these third generation Transporters were made in Germany until July 1990, in Austria until September 1992, in Malaysia until 1995, and are still currently in production in South Africa.

24 - Single or double cab pick-up
25 - Panel van; Kombi (window van); Ambulance; Bus; Bus L; Caravelle CL, GL and Carat.

Brazilian Bay-window Bus/T2 (1976-date)

20 - Microbus
21 - Panel van
23 - Kombi (window van)
26 - Single or double cab pick-up
27 - Ambulance (made by Karmann-Ghia do Brasil)

CHASSIS NUMBERS & REAR/FRONT AXLE CODING
1950 – 1968

It is interesting to note that a full listing of the earliest Split-screen Bus transmission part numbers is difficult to find, until you realise that these were essentially modified Beetle items, with only the rear axle, reduction gear housings and the gears themselves having separate part numbers. During the 1959 year (from chassis number 469 506), the fully synchronised transmission and rear axle assembly received its own part number. The following lists mirror VW's own internal publication called 'Progressive Refinements', and the 'Technical Bulletins' issued to VW dealers to identify major components, but cannot be considered totally complete, as some variations are apparent between lists. The numbers are related to chassis numbers and/or year-end dates (or dates when substantial technical innovations were introduced) to aid ease of identification.

Year	Chassis No	Front axle	Rear axle
Mar 50	20-000 001	-	168 255
(1st T'porter 8.3.50)			
Apr 50	20- 000 372	-	174 872
Dec 50	20- 008 112	-	244 739
Jan 51	20- 009 542	-	255 108
Dec 51	20- 020 112	-	357 345
Jan 52	20- 021 347	2-021 617	367 597
Aug 52	20- 032 823	2-033 246	443 360
Sept 52	20- 035 134	2-035 560	A-1 227 456 613
Dec 52	20- 041 857	2-042 283	A-24 736 469 555
Jan 53	20- 044 361	2-044 828	A-35 618 473 255
Dec 53	20- 070 431	2-071 020	A-172 034 503 903
Jan 54	20- 073 148	2-073 968	A-186 768 506 934
Dec 54	20-110 603	2-111 670	A-380 323 538 982
Jan 55	20-114 525	2-115 620	A-401 939 542 325
Dec 55	20-160 735	2-162 204	A-677 497 573 609
Jan 56	165 518	2-167 114	A-708 286 576 517
Dec 56	223 216	2-226 147	A-1 044 024 613 554
Jan 57	230 857	2-233 936	A-1 082 258 616 471
Dec 57	315 209	2-317 251	A-1 488 444 640 822
Jan 58	324 344	2-327 053	A-1 537 488 643 226
Dec 58	416 082	2-427 875	A-2 027 204 664 479
Jan 59	433 713	2-437 635	A-2 079 110 666 409
Apr 59	465 351	2-466 864	B-2 240 909 671 767
Dec 59	546 843	2-547 836	B-2 712 903 685 788
Jan 60	566 342	2-559 234	B-2 780 435 687 705
Apr 60	601 918	2-594 707	B-3 005 555 693 122
Dec 60	710 069	2-688 468	B-3 637 181 703 268
Jan 61	723 431	2-703 943	B-3 728 422 704 331
May 61	784 276	2-758 463	B-4 044 033 709 158
Dec 61	882 314	2-840 894	B-4 458 031 718 205
Jan 62	896 977	2-855 335	-
Sep 62 (new mdl.yr.)	1 004 496	2-962 664	-
Dec 62	1 047 967	1 006 544	-
1962 (yr.end)	1 048 085	1 007 922	-5 535 965
Jan 63	1 062 951	1 020 900	-

Dec 63	1 222 500	1 184 507	-
Jan 64	1 241 702	1 203 708	-
Jul 64	1 328 871	1 295 803	-
Aug 64 (new mdl.yr.)	215 019 888	1 310 508	-
Dec 64	215 082 480	1 373 451	-
Jan 65	215 098 657	1 388 657	-
Jul 65	215 176 339	1 471 307	-
Aug 65 (new mdl.yr.)	216 020 494	-	-
Dec 65	216 083 207	8 707 954	-
Jan 66	216 098 498	-	-
Jul 66	216 179 668	-	-
Aug 66 (new mdl.yr.)	217 020 467	-	-
Dec 66	217 079 889	-	-
Jan 67	217 091 416	-	-
Jul 67	217 148 549	-	-
Aug 67 (new mdl.yr.)	218 011 837	-	-
Dec 67	218 073 585	-	-
Jan 68	218 092 976	-	-
Jul 68	218 202 251	-	-
Aug 68 (new mdl.yr.)	219 017 255	-	-
Dec 68	219 098 974	-	-

TRANSMISSION (FULLY SYNCHRONISED), FROM CHASSIS 469 506

Part No.	Description
211 300 025 G	Transmission and rear axle assembly from chassis 614 456 up to 1 144 281
211 300 025 K	Transmission and rear axle assembly from chassis 1 144 282 up to 215 035 227
211 300 025 L	Transmission and rear axle assembly up to chassis 216 190 000
211 300 025 M	Transmission and rear axle assembly from chassis 217 000 001
211 300 043 A	Transmission from chassis 469 506 up to 215 035 227
211 300 043 C	Transmission up to chassis 216 190 000
211 300 043 G	Transmission from chassis 217 000 001

REAR AXLES

Since November 1964, rear axles with optional extras (M) have been marked after the rear axle numbers as follows:
Rear axles with limited slip differential (M220) with an 'S'
Rear axles with mountain ratios (M 92) with an 'M'
Rear axles with limited slip and mountain ratios with 'SM'
The rear axle number is stamped on the right side of the transmission housing seen from the driving direction.

REAR AXLE SHAFT

Part No.	
211 501 201	Rear axle shaft
	003 - pink
	002 - green (colour code)

REDUCTION GEARS

Gear ratio Type 2/1200cc   1.39:1   number of teeth 25/18
Gear ratio Type 2/1500cc and 1 ton   1.26:1   number of teeth 24/19

REDUCTION GEAR HOUSINGS

Part No.
211 501 235   left gear housing, up to chassis 20-117 901
211 501 236   right gear housing, up to chassis 20-117 901
181 501 237   left gear housing, from chassis 20-117 902 up to 1 144 281
181 501 238   right gear housing, from chassis 20-117 902 up to 1 144 281
211 501 237 D   left gear housing from chassis 1 144 282 (M216)
211 501 238 D   right gear housing from chassis 1 144 282 (M216)

GEARS

Part No.
211 501 261 A   gear - rear axle shaft (18 teeth) up to chassis 215 036 650
(up to chassis 469 505, use 211 501 267 B)

211 501 261 A   gear - rear axle shaft (18 teeth- modified ratio for mountainous districts) up to chassis 215 036 650 (M92/M215, M216) from chassis 215 036 651 (on type M92)

211 501 261 B   gear - rear axle shaft (16 teeth - modified ratio for mountainous districts) from chassis 20-117 902 to 1 222 025 (M92)

211 501 261 C   gear - rear axle shaft (19 teeth) up to chassis 215 036 650 (M216, M216), from chassis 215 036 651

DRIVEN GEAR & SHAFT

Part No.
211 501 267B   Driven gear and shaft (25 teeth) from chassis 20-117 902 up to 1 144 281 (up to chassis 469 505 use 211 501 261 A)

211 501 267 C   Driven gear and shaft (27 teeth) modified ratio for mountainous districts, from chassis 20 - 117 902 up to 1 144 281. Type M92.

211 501 267 J   Driven gear and shaft (25 teeth) modified ratio for mountainous districts, up to chassis 1 144 281. Type M92/M216

211 501 267 D   Driven gear and shaft (25 teeth) up to chassis 20 - 117 901
211 501 267 H   Driven gear and shaft (24 teeth) up to chassis 1 144 281. Type M216
211 501 267 K   Driven gear and shaft (24 teeth) from chassis 1 144 282 up to 215 036 650. Type M215/M216 from chassis 215 036 651
211 501 267 L   Driven gear and shaft (25 teeth) from chassis 1 144 282 up to 215 036 650
211 501 267 L   Driven gear and shaft (25 teeth) modified ratio for mountainous driving from chassis 1 144 282 up to 215 036 650. Type M92/M215, M216 from chassis 215 036 651
211 501 267 M   Driven gear and shaft (27 teeth) modified ratio for mountainous districts from chassis 1 144 282 up to 1 222 025. Type M92

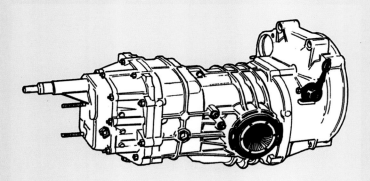

T2 AND T3 TRANSPORTER TRANSMISSION CODES
August 1968 - July 2002

The information in this list is derived from a number of sources including the official Volkswagen Parts List CD-ROM (ETKA) (Europe) dated July 2000. The assistance of Harald Holecek of Graz, Austria is also gratefully acknowledged. Every effort has been made to attain accuracy and the wording has been chosen very carefully. It covers VW Transporter T2 and T3 models manufactured at Hanover in Germany. It also covers VW Transporter T2 ("Bay-window") models manufactured and CKD assembled in Australia, Ireland and South Africa as well as Transporter T3 models manufactured in Austria and South Africa. It does not cover VW Transporter T1 ("Split-screen") models made in Germany, Australia, Brazil and South Africa. It also does not cover VW Transporter T2 models made in Mexico until 1997 and Transporter T2 models still currently made in Brazil. It does not cover the current German range of Type 70 or Transporter T4 models with transverse front engine and front-wheel-drive.

Code	Dates	Transporter version	Manual/Automatic	CPR	Engine/Comments
CA	8/67-7/70	T2	Manual 4	5.429	1600
CB	8/70-7/73	T2	Manual 4	5.429	1600
CC	8/70-7/71	T2	Manual 4	5.429	1600
CD	8/70-7/73	T2	Manual 4	5.429	1600
CE	8/73-8/75	T2	Manual 4	5.429	1600
CF	8/73-8/75	T2	Manual 4	5.429	1600
CG	8/71-7/75	T2	Manual 4	5.429	1600 M-220
CH	8/71-7/75	T2	Manual 4	5.857	1600 M-092
CK	8/71-12/73	T2	Manual 4	5.429	1600
CL	8/71-12/73	T2	Manual 4	5.429	1700
CM	8/73-7/74	T2	Manual 4	4.857	1800
CN	8/73-7/75	T2	Manual 4	4.857	1800 M-220
CP	8/75-7/79	T2	Manual 4	4.571	2000
CT	8/75-7/79	T2	Manual 4	4.571	2000 M-220
CU	9/75-7/79	T2	Manual 4	5.429	1600
CV	9/75-7/79	T2	Manual 4	5.429	1600 M-220
CW	9/75-7/79	T2	Manual 4	5.857	1600 M-092
CX	9/75-7/79	T2	Manual 4	5.429	1600
DE	8/67-7/75	T2	Manual 4	5.429	1600
DH	1/81-12/82	T3	Manual 4	5.428	1600/T3

DJ	1/81-12/82	T3	Manual 4	5.86	2000
DK	5/79-12/82	T3 USA/CDN	Manual 4	4.571	2000
DL	8/79-12/82	T3	Manual 4	4.571	2000
DM	8/81-10/81	T3 USA/CDN	Manual 4	5.43	Diesel
DN	9/79-12/82	T3	Manual 4	5.86	1600/T3
DP	5/79-12/82	T3	Manual 4	4.57	2000
DO	5/79-12/82	T3	Manual 4	5.86	1600/T3
	1/81-12/82	T3 Campmobile	Manual 4	5.86	1600/T3
DR	8/79-12/82	T3	Manual 4	4.86	2000
DS	8/82-9/83	T3	Manual 4	5.43	Diesel
DT	8/82-7/84	T3	Manual 4	4.57	WBX1.9
DU	1/83-7/84	T3 USA/CDN'	Manual 4	4.86	WBX1.9
DV	8/82-9/83	T3 Campmobile,	Manual 5	4.86	WBX1.9
	8/82-7/84	T3	Manual 5	4.86	WBX1.9
DW	8/82-9/83	T3	Manual 5	4.86	WBX1.9
DX	8/82-9/83	T3	Manual 5	5.43	Diesel
	8/82-9/83	T3 USA/CDN	Manual 5	5.43	Diesel
DY	6/82-3/84	T3	Manual 4	5.86	Diesel
DZ	10/81-6/82	T3 USA/CDN	Manual 4	5.86	Diesel
FF	8/82-8/92	T3	Automatic	4.09	WBX 1.9
FFA	8/82-8/92	T3	Automatic	4.09	WBX 1.9
NA	8/71-12/73	T2	Automatic	4.26	1700
NB	8/71-7/75	T2	Automatic	4.26	1700, 1800
NC	3/74-7/74	T2	Automatic	4.26	1800
ND	9/74-7/75	T2	Automatic	4.26	1800
NE	8/76-6/77	T2	Automatic	4.26	2000
NF	8/76-6/77	T2	Automatic	4.26	2000
NG	5/79-12/82	T3 USA/CDN	Automatic	4.09	2000
NH	8/82-7/91	T3 Campmobile	Automatic	4.09	WBX 1.9
	8/82-7/85	T3	Automatic	4.09	WBX 1.9
	8/84-7/85	T3 Vanagon	Automatic	4.09	WBX 1.9
NJ	8/85-7/91	T3 Campmobile	Automatic	3.74	WBX 1.9, 2.1
	8/84-7/85	T3	Automatic	3.74	WBX 1.9, 2.1
NK	8/86-7/89	T3	Automatic	4.09	WBX 2.1
	8/88-7/92	T3 Vanagon	Automatic	4.09	WBX 2.1
NL	8/86-7/89	T3 Campmobile	Automatic	4.09	WBX 1.9, 2.1
	8/87-7/89	T3	Automatic	4.09	WBX 1.9, 2.1
NM	8/86-7/91	T3	Automatic	4.09	WBX 2.1 M-523 taxi
AAK	8/84-7/85	T3 Campmobile	Syncro 4+G	4.86	WBX 1.9, 2.1
	2/85-7/87	T3	Syncro 4+G	4.86	WBX 1.9, 2.1
	8/85-7/86	T3 Vanagon	Syncro 4+G	4.86	WBX 1.9
AAL	4/89-7/91	T3 Engageable 4WD (4+G)		4.86	WBX 1.9, 2.1
AAM	4/89-7/91	T3 Engageable 4WD (4+G)		4.86	WBX 1.9, 2.1 + diff lock
AAN	8/85-7/89	T3 Campmobile	Syncro 4+G	4.86	WBX 1.9, 2.1 + diff lock
	1/86-7/92	T3	Syncro 4+G	4.86	WBX 1.9, 2.1 + diff lock
	8/85-7/86	T3 Vanagon	Syncro 4+G	4.86	WBX 2.1 + diff lock
AAP	8/85-7/91	T3 Campmobile	Manual 5	4.57	WBX 2.1

	8/84-7/85	T3	Manual 5	4.57	WBX 1.9, 2.1
AAR	8/85-7/91	T3 Campmobile	Manual 5	4.57	WBX 1.9, 2.1
	8/84-7/85	T3	Manual 5	4.57	WBX 1.9, 2.1
AAS	8/85-7/91	T3 Campmobile	Manual 5	4.83	1.6TD
	8/87-7/92	T3	Manual 5	4.83	1.6TD
ABB	8/84-7/91	T3 Campmobile	Manual 4	4.57	WBX 1.9
	8/84-7/85	T3	Manual 4	4.57	WBX 1.9
ABD	8/85-12/85	T3 Campmobile	Manual 4	4.83	WBX 1.9
	8/84-7/85	T3 Vanagon	Manual 4	4.83	WBX 1.9
ABE	8/86-10/88	T3 Campmobile	Manual 4	4.83	WBX 1.9
	8/85-7/87	T3	Manual 4	4.83	WBX 1.9
ABF	8/84-12/86	T3 Campmobile	Manual 4	5.83	Diesel
	8/86-7/85	T3	Manual 4	5.83	Diesel
ABH	8/84-7/91	T3 Campmobile	Manual 5	5.5	1.6TD
	8/84-7/85	T3	Manual 5	5.5	1.6TD
ABK	8/87-7/89	T3	Manual 5	4.83	WBX 2.1
ABL	8/84-7/89	T3 Campmobile	Manual 5	4.83	WBX 1.9
	8/84-7/85	T3	Manual 5	4.83	WBX 1.9/
ABM	8/84-7/85	T3 Campmobile	Manual 5	4.83	WBX 1.9
	7/89-7/92	T3	Manual 5	4.83	WBX 1.9
ABN	8/84-7/85	T3	Manual 5	4.83	WBX 1.9
ABP	10/84-7/85	T3	Manual 5	5.5	Diesel
ABR	8/84-7/91	T3 Campmobile	Manual 5	5.5	Diesel
	8/84-7/85	T3	Manual 5	5.5	Diesel
ABS	1/86-7/91	T3 Campmobile	Manual 4	5.43	Diesel
	1/86-7/92	T3	Manual 4	5.43	Diesel
ACP	3/84-7/84	T3 Campmobile	Manual 4	5.83	Diesel
ACR	3/84-7/84	T3 Campmobile	Manual 4	5.83	Diesel
ACU	8/85-7/86	T3 Campmobile	Automatic	4.86	WBX 1.9, 2.1
	8/85-7/92	T3	Automatic	4.86	WBX 1.9, 2.1
	8/85-7/86	T3 Vanagon	Automatic	4.86	WBX 2.1
ACW	8/88-7/91	T3 Campmobile	Manual 4	4.83	WBX 1.9, 2.1
	8/88-7/92	T3	Manual 4	4.83	WBX 1.9, 2.1
	8/87-7/92	T3 Vanagon	Manual 4	4.83	WBX 2.1
ADH	8/86-7/87	T3 Campmobile	Automatic	4.86	WBX 1.9, 2.1
	8/85-7/87	T3	Automatic	4.86	WBX 1.9, 2.1
	8/85-7/86	T3 Vanagon	Automatic	4.86	WBX 2.1
ADM	8/85-7/91	T3 Campmobile	Automatic	5.43	WBX 1.9, 2.1
	1/86-7/87	T3	Automatic	5.43	WBX 1.9, 2.1
	8/85-7/86	T3 Vanagon	Automatic/	5.43	WBX 2.1
AFJ	8/91-present	T3 Microbus/Caravelle	Manual 5	4.83	2.3, 2.5-litre 5-cyl (S. Africa)
AGT	8/86-7/91	T3 Campmobile	Manual 5	4.83	WBX 2.1
	8/85-7/92	T3	Manual 5	4.83	WBX 2.1
AGZ	8/86-7/87	T3 Campmobile	Syncro 4+G	5.43	1.6TD
	4/86-8/89	T3	Syncro 4+G	5.43	1.6TD
AHA	4/89-8/89	T3	Syncro 4+G	5.83	1.6TD
AHB	4/89-7/91	T3 Campmobile	Automatic	5.83	WBX 2.1
	4/89-7/92	T3	Automatic	5.83	WBX 2.1

	4/89-7/91	T3 Vanagon	Automatic	5.83	WBX 2.1
AHF	8/86-7/86	T3 Campmobile	Syncro 4+G	5.43	1.6TD + diff lock
	3/86 8/89	T3	Syncro 4+G	5.43	1.6TD + diff lock
AHT	7/87-7/91	T3 Campmobile	Automatic	5.83	WBX 1.9, 2.1
	7/87-7/92	T3	Automatic	5.83	WBX 1.9, 2.1
	7/87-7/89	T3 Vanagon	Automatic	5.83	WBX 2.1
AHU	7/87-7/91	T3 Campmobile	Automatic	5.83	WBX 1.9, 2.1
	7/87-7/92	T3 Vanagon	Automatic	5.83	WBX 2.1
AHX	7/87-7/92	T3	Syncro 4+G	4.57	WBX 1.9 Power take-off
AKE	1/87-8/89	T3	Syncro 4+G	4.57	WBX 1.9, 2.1
	1/87-7/89	T3 Vanagon	Syncro 4+G	4.57	WBX 2.1
AKF	8/86-7/87	T3 Campmobile	Automatic	4.57	WBX 2.1
	11/86-7/92	T3 Vanagon	Automatic	4.57	WBX 2,1
AKG	8/86-7/87	T3 Campmobile	Syncro 4+G	4.57	WBX 2.1 + diff lock
	11/86-7/89	T3 Vanagon	Syncro 4+G	4.57	WBX 2.1 + diff lock
AKH	8/86-7/87	T3 Campmobile	Automatic	4.57	WBX 1.9, 2.1
	7/87-7/89	T3	Automatic	4.57	WBX 1.9, 2.1
	7/87-7/92	T3 Vanagon	Automatic	4.57	WBX 2.1
AKK	4/89-8/89	T3	Syncro 4+G	5.83	1.6TD
	8/85-8/89	T3 Vanagon	Syncro 4+G	5.83	1.6TD
ALD	8/87-7/88	T3	Manual 4	5.5	Diesel
	10/86-7/91	T3 Campmobile	Manual 4	5.5	Diesel
ALE	4/89-8/89	T3	Syncro 4+G	5.83	WBX 2.1 + diff lock 16"
ALK	7/87-8/89	T3	Syncro 4+G	5.43	WBX 2.1 + diff lock 16"
ALM	4/89-7/92	T3	Automatic	5.83	WBX 2.1
ALN	4/89-7/92	T3	Automatic	5.83	WBX 2.1
ANB	1/88-7/89	T3	Automatic	6.17	WBX 2.1
ANC	1/88-7/92	T3	Automatic	6.17	1.6TD
AND	1/88-8/89	T3	Syncro 4+G	6.17	1.6TD + diff lock 16"
AND	1/88-8/89	T3	Syncro 4+G	6.17	WBX 2.1 + diff lock 16"
AOJ	8/88-3/00	T3	Manual 4	4.83	1.8-litre 4-cyl (S. Africa)
AOK	8/94-present	T3 Microbus	Manual 4	4.83	2.6-litre 5-cyl (S. Africa)
AOL	1/88-7/92	T3	Automatic	6.17	WBX 2.1
AOM	1/88-7/92	T3	Automatic	6.17	WBX 2.1
APF	8/87-7/89	T3	Manual 4	5.5	Diesel
ASL	8/88-7/91	T3 Campmobile	Manual 5	4.57	WBX 2.1
	8/88-7/92	T3	Manual 5	4.57	WBX 2.1
ASM	8/88-7/91	T3 Campmobile	Manual 5	4.57	WBX 2.1
	8/89-7/92	T3	Manual 5	4.57	WBX 2.1
ASN	8/89-7/91	T3 Campmobile	Manual 5	5.5	Diesel
	8/89-7/92	T3	Manual 5	5.5	Diesel
ASP	8/89-7/91	T3 Campmobile	Manual 5	5.5	Diesel
	8/89-7/92	T3	Manual 5	5.5	Diesel
ASR	7/89-7/91	T3 Campmobile	Manual 5	4.83	1.6TD
	7/89-7/92	T3	Manual 5	4.83	1.6TD
ASS	7/89-7/91	T3 Campmobile	Manual 5	4.83	1.6TD
	7/89-7/92	T3	Manual 5	4.83	1.6TD
AST	8/88-7/91	T3 Campmobile	Manual 5	4.57	WBX 2.1

	8/88-7/92	T3	Manual 5	4.57	WBX 2.1
AVF	9/89-7/92	T3	Syncro 4+G	5.83	1.6TD
AVH	9/89-7/91	T3 Campmobile	Syncro 4+G	5.43	WBX 1.9, 2.1
	9/89-7/92	T3 Vanagon	Syncro 4+G	5.43	WBX 2.1
AVJ	9/89-7/92	T2	Syncro 4+G	5.43	1.6TD
AVK	9/89-7/92	T2	Syncro 4+G	5.43	1.6TD + diff lock
AVL	9/89-7/91	T3 Campmobile	Syncro 4+G	5.43	WBX 1.9, 2.1 + diff lock
	9/89-7/92	T3 Vanagon	Syncro 4+G	5.43	WBX 2.1 + diff lock
AVM	9/89-7/92	T3	Syncro 4+G	5.83	WBX 1.9, 2.1 + difflock 16"
AVN	9/89-7/91	T3 Campmobile	Syncro 4+G	4.86	WBX 1.9, 2.1 + diff lock
	9/89-7/91	T3	Syncro 4+G	4.86	WBX 2.1 + diff lock 16"
	9/89-7/91	T3	Syncro 4+G	4.86	WBX 1.9, 2.1 + diff lock
	9/89-7/92	T3 Vanagon	Syncro 4+G	4.86	WBX 2.1 + diff lock
AVR	9/89-7/92	T3	Syncro 4+G	5.83	WBX 2.1 + diff lock 16"
AVS	9/89-7/92	T3	Syncro 4+G	5.83	16TD + diff lock
AVU	9/87-7/92	T3	Syncro 4+G	6.17	1.6TD + diff lock 16"
AVV	9/89-7/91	T3 Campmobile	Syncro 4+G	4.86	WBX 1.9, 2.1
	9/89-7/92	T3 Vanagon	Syncro 4+G	4.86	WBX 2.1
2D	8/84-7/91	T3	Manual 5	5.86	Diesel
3H	8/84-7/91	T3 Campmobile	Manual 5	4.83	Diesel
	8/87-7/92	T3	Manual 5	4.83	Diesel
3P	10/83-7/84	T3 Campmobile	Manual 5	4.86	WBX 1.9
	1/83-7/84	T3	Manual 5	4.86	WBX 1.9
4D	8/82-7/84	T3	Manual 4	4.57	WBX 1.9
5D	8/82-7/84	T3	Manual 4	4.86	WBX 1.9
6D	6/82-3/84	T3	Manual 4	5.86	Diesel
6N	8/85-7/86	T3 Campmobile	Automatic	5.43	WBX 2.1
	8/86-7/89	T3	Automatic	5.43	WBX 2.1
	8/85-7/86	T3 Vanagon	Automatic	5.43	WBX 2.1
6P	8/86-7/87	T3 Campmobile	Syncro 4+G	5.43	WBX 1.9, 2.1
	8/85-7/89	T3	Syncro 4+G	5.43	WBX 1.9, 2.1
	8/85-7/86	T3 Vanagon	Syncro 4+G	5.43	WBX 2.1
6PA	8/87-7/91	T3 Campmobile	Syncro 4+G	5.43	WBX 1.9, 2.1 + diff lock
	8/87-7/92	T3	Syncro 4+G	5.43	WBX 1.9, 2.1 + diff lock
	8/87-7/89	T3 Vanagon	Syncro 4+G	5.43	WBX 2.1 + diff lock
6ZA	2/85-7/85	T3 Engageable 4WD (4+G)		5.43	WBX 1.9, 2.1 + diff lock
6Z	2/85-7/85	T3 Engageable 4WD (4+G)		5.43	WBX 1.9, 2.1
7D	8/82-9/83	T3	Manual 5	4.86	WBX 1.9
8D	8/82-9/83	T3	Manual 5	4.86	WBX 1.9
8E	10/83-7/84	T3	Manual 5	4.86	WBX 1.9
8F	10/83-7/84	T3	Manual 5	4.86	WBX 1.9
8H	10/83-7/84	T3	Manual 5	4.86	WBX 1.9
8K	10/83-7/84	T3	Manual 5	5.43	Diesel
8L	10/83-7/84	T3	Manual 5	5.43	Diesel
9D	8/82-9/83	T3	Manual 5	5.43	Diesel

Note: WBX = waserboxer/water-cooled engine
Syncro 4+G = full-time 4-wheel drive, 4 speed manual gearbox plus low gear and viscous front differential.

MAXIMUM RECOMMENDED FRONT SUSPENSION ADJUSTMENTS

(from stock set screw location, using an adjustment system such as Bus Boys Albatross adjusters)

Split-screen Bus/T1	(1950 –1967)	Lowering	- 4 increments (24)
		Raising	- 6 increments (36)
Bay-window Bus/T2	(1968 - 1969)	Lowering	- 6 increments (36)
		Raising	- 4 increments (24)
	(1970 - 1979)	Lowering	- 7 increments (42)
		Raising	- 3 increments (18)

One increment of adjustment is a 6 change. Beyond these ranges, the body will interfere with steering components, and require additional work to allow these components to function safely. The bump stops will need to be relocated to prevent excessive trailing arm movement, but ideally should not be removed from the front suspension.

GLOSSARY OF TERMS

English	American	English	American	English	American
Accelerator	Gas pedal	Gearbox	Transmission	Steering arm	Spindle arm
Anti-roll bar	Stabiliser or sway bar	Gearchange	Shift	Swarf	Metal chips
		Halfshaft/driveshaft	Axle shaft	Track rod	Tie rod
Battery	Energizer	Handbrake	Parking brake	Trailing shoe	Secondary shoe
Bodywork	Sheet metal	Leading shoe	Primary shoe		
Bulkhead	Firewall	Microbus	Station wagon	Transmission	Whole driveline
Bush	Bushing	Petrol	Gasoline	Tyre	Tire
Circlip	Snap-ring	Petrol tank	Gas tank	Van	Panel wagon/ van
Clearance	Lash	Seized	Frozen		
Damper	Shock absorber	Sill panel	Rocker panel	Vice	Vise
Disc	Rotor/disk	Spanner	Wrench	Wheel nut	Lug nut
Drop arm	Pitman arm	Split pin	Cotter pin	Windscreen	Windshield

Bluebird Customs

Est 1978

32 Whalley Rd Gt Harwood Lanc's BB6 7TF-01254 888416-www.bluebird-type2.co.uk-foksy@freenetname.co.uk

The Foksy type 2 front beam adjuster, allows easy adjustment of front ride height £ 85.95

Underdash parcel trays fits all bays mesh type as original....£ 49.95

13 Watt folding solar panel

Great for keeping your battery topped up during a long stay or winter layoff. comes with all cables and built in supports. Gives out approx 1.08 amp/hour. a very usefull bit of kit £103.50

Cab Bunk fits splits, bays & T25's full kit with telescopic poles for easy storage £59.95

Type 2 urethene rear spring plate bushes set of 4 £ 35.00

Jail bars £ 49.95 set polished aluminium

Stainless steel BBQ two cooking surfaces compact when packed £ 39.95

Spare wheel cover No 8 £ 21.95

Side step.cast/extruded in alluminium fits into jacking points on splits & bays. £ 145.00

Rock & roll Beds from £ 195.00

Electrolux 2 and 3 way Refrigerators From £ 289.95

Rear mounted spare wheel carrier, mounts to rear bumper £ 79.95

Insulated screen cover £39.95

Performance stainless system 1600 > single quiet pack complete with gaskets & fitting kit £ 225.00

Buddy seats from £45.00

Stock style stainless system inc fitting kit £ 225.00

Stainless Vent Shades fit all bay cab doors £ 29.95 pair

Pendle bike racks from £ 80.00

Pop out rear cargo window, complete kit. £165.00

Propex Heatsource £425.00

Manufactured exclusivley for us by a leading tent manufacturer. Deluxe Freestanding awning 3mx3mx2m tall yet packs small. internal silver coating reflects light. comes with twin size inner sleep tent pegs.guys.and sill to floor draught excluder.fits all vans. Taped seams ripstop polyester. £ 225.00

12v low energy awning lights each light consumes approx 5 watt & gives out approx 70 watt of light.Complete withfitted cigarette plug & 8 metres of cable £ 29.95

Sun Shady heavy duty gray fabric,fully waterproof Clips into gutter . Complete with adjustable poles, guy lines & pegs £ 95.00

Prices include VAT and shipping UK mainland

See more at our online shop www.bluebird-type2.co.uk

Index